Crosscurrents / MODERN CRITIQUES

Harry T. Moore, *General Editor*

The Hellenism
of MARY RENAULT

Bernard F. Dick

WITH A PREFACE BY
Harry T. Moore

SOUTHERN ILLINOIS UNIVERSITY PRESS
Carbondale and Edwardsville

FEFFER & SIMONS, INC.
London and Amsterdam

For
Gilbert Highet

Contents

The Hellenism of Mary Renault takes us into the realm of the historical novel. Recently a writer in a national magazine, in discussing The Conspiracy, by John Hersey —a better-than-usual Hersey, set in Nero's Rome—mentioned a group of outstanding writers of fiction about the ancient world, of course including Robert Graves. He spoke of Mary Renault, among others, but also dragged in Gore Vidal (why?). Further, this reviewer omitted Thornton Wilder's The Ides of March, a fine novel in itself and one which gave direct ancestry to Hersey's book, which is mostly a matter of letters exchanged, reports of interrogations, and so on. The reviewer didn't even refer in passing to Walter Pater's Marius the Epicurean, but perhaps he is just too young to know such books, even Wilder's comparatively recent Ides.

This brings us to the question: What is a historical novel, and which is the best of them? One title, which has no connection with the ancient world, springs to mind at once: Tolstoy's War and Peace. True, it deals with events only a generation or so earlier, but Tolstoy's researches, into events at the time of the Napoleonic wars and even into his own family records, make him a historical novelist—among so much else. One wonders how that once-famous book, Charles Kingsley's The Cloister and the Hearth—which in any event couldn't be classed with Tolstoy's book—would fare in a reading today.

But I have no doubts about George Moore's Héloïse and Abélard, which is still kept in print in America, by Liveright. Too few readers know of this book, which I place as the greatest of historical novels (if we exclude Tolstoy's War and Peace, which is so much more than merely "historical"). Héloïse and Abélard is, among other things, superbly written. It tells a powerful story of forbidden love and its disastrous aftermath. The book projects medieval Paris wonderfully (one thinks of Robert Louis Stevenson's fine story of François Villion in "A Lodging for the Night"). And George Moore adds greatly to the story in its presentation of the beginnings of the Children's Crusade. Another important matter is the disputes of the Schoolmen, a significant part of the story, again supremely "done." Such books show us how viable the historical novel can be.

In our time we have had, besides Wilder, such excellent examples of the genre as the late Alfred Duggan and Mary Renault (whose real name is Mary Challans). Miss Renault's main fictional concern is Hellenism, though she gets into what is known, in contradistinction, as the Hellenistic period when she writes about Alexander the Great. She deals with him in Fire From Heaven, which at this writing is her latest novel; the present study is the first to deal with it. Also, two of Miss Renault's other books, The King Must Die and Bull from the Sea, are set in pre-Hellenic Minoan civilization. But her books all through her career reflect the ideals of the Hellenic civilization, none more so than The Charioteer, which has a twentieth-century setting yet is imbued with Hellenic philosophy.

The author of this book on Mary Renault, Bernard F. Dick, teaches at Fairleigh Dickinson University. Most of his work is in English literature, but from time to time he gives courses in Greek civilization. For the present book he read all the sources listed in Mary Renault's novels, and he has carried on an extensive correspondence with her while writing this volume. All these activities contribute toward making this study one of high quality indeed.

Professor Dick begins with a thorough scrutiny of Miss Renault's early novels, so important for a true understanding of the later works. These he deals with in depth, in a very interesting fashion which will have the double effect of driving new readers to Mary Renault's books and of illuminating them for those who have already read them.

Miss Renault brings a world to life in her novels, and Bernard F. Dick helps importantly to a fuller understanding of them, by providing not only interpretation and criticism, but also discussions of myth, which Mary Renault handles with such skill.

HARRY T. MOORE

Southern Illinois University
March 17, 1972

Introduction

If one were to mention the name of Mary Renault (pseudonym of Mary Challans) to a specialist in contemporary fiction, he would probably nod affirmatively and cite *The Last of the Wine* or *The King Must Die* as proof of his familiarity with her work. If the specialist were asked why she is one of the most widely read novelists among university types but one of the least written about, he would no doubt suggest that the current critical preoccupation with the mythic novel, the nonnovel, the antinovel, and the black novel leaves little room for the historical which everyone knows is *vulgarisation*. He might also argue that Mary Renault fictionalizes material with which many literary critics would be uncomfortable: "Who but the classicist, or possibly the comparatist, is conversant enough with Greek civilization to speak with any authority about her books? It was difficult enough reviewing Anthony Burgess's *Nothing Like the Sun* when one had not thought about sonnet sequences since graduate school."

Like the culture about which she writes, Mary Renault is both admired and ignored. As a historical novelist, she will never attract the cultists unless there is a revival of interest in Bulwer-Lytton. While her ability to fictionalize the past has excluded her from the corps of "serious" writers, it has made her one of the most popular novelists of the mid-twentieth century. Mary Renault is also a writer of best sellers, two of which were sold to the movies but never filmed: *Return to Night* which won the Metro-Goldwyn-Mayer Award of $150,000 in 1947, and *The King Must Die* which Twentieth Century Fox purchased after its publication in 1958.

Mary Renault's popularity among the Book-of-the-Month Club membership has undoubtedly handicapped her among the scholars who write for the quarterlies. While it is usually true that the American best seller is inferior art, there have been those happy exceptions— Muriel Spark's *The Mandelbaum Gate*, Vladimir Nabokov's *Ada*, John Fowles's *The Frencr Lieutenant's Woman*, Eudora Welty's *Losing Battles*—which augur well for literacy. Mary Renault is obviously not for the Jacqueline Susann-Harold Robbins trade. She has attracted two types of readers: fiction lovers who know little about the Hellenic past but who appreciate a novel with linear narration, a well-constructed plot, and an antique flavor; and the students of literature who, like the theatregoers in Periclean Athens, enjoy seeing what new insights an author can bring to decisive events like the Peloponnesian War, historical figures like Socrates and Alexander the Great, and mythological ones like Theseus and Phaedra.

The Hellenism of Mary Renault is primarily an attempt to show how a former nurse who wrote women's fiction during World War II has managed to re-create the ethos, ideology, and even the language patterns of a world that is completely removed from the present. Secondly, it is an attempt to justify historical fiction, a genre which is so often misunderstood because it is so often abused.

The term "historical novelist" usually evokes the names of writers like Taylor Caldwell, Thomas B. Costain, and Frank Yerby, all of whom have resurrected the past with more fancy than scholarship. Mary Renault is also a historical novelist; unfortunately, she belongs to a genre which has traditionally involved more craft than art. Moreover, there have been few quality writers of this school; one thinks immediately of Scott and Bulwer-Lytton, less immediately of G. P. R. James and William Ainsworth. Scott's case is typical of the historical novelist's plight. E. M. Forster's verdict, "a trivial mind and a heavy style," was pithy enough to leave its mark. In *The Living Novel*, V. S. Pritchett admirably defended Scott against Forster's charge that he lacked "passion" by showing that his passion was something historical, a "preoccupation with what is settled," rather than a rhapsodic oneness with glens and lovers which seems to be what Forster would have preferred.

Mary Renault's passion also lies in history—in the ebb and flow of accidents and essences, the web of conjectures, the sources that complement and contradict, the anecdotes so time-honored that their original meaning was never questioned. Like Scott, she will not refrain from using the supernatural as an index of religious belief and as a vehicle for characterization. Unlike Scott who was often inaccurate, Mary Renault researches her novels with a peerless *Wissenschaft*, even drawing on the findings of archaeology for a description of a talisman, a hair style, a snake-headed ship, or the décor of a child's bedroom in Minoan Crete.

This scholarly approach to historical fiction sets her apart from other exponents of the genre who think in terms of film rights and consequently produce a skeletal scenario where battles, lovemaking, duels, and sieges are described so generally that they could fit just about any era. Mary Renault does not write cinematically in her Greek novels, although once or twice in her early fiction she did shoot scenes instead of constructing episodes. What is unique about Mary Renault is a methodology that should endear her to academicians, for she is the only novelist writing historical fiction today who approaches her material from the standpoint of a scholar.

Her Greek novels usually contain endpaper maps, a selected bibliography, and an Author's Note explaining how she used her primary sources. Contrary to what many readers suppose, the interpretative essay and the bibliography were the author's idea, not her publisher's. In a letter (July 9, 1970) she clarified her rationale for me: "I think one has a duty to the uninformed reader to tell him when one is giving him authentic history and when one is making it up. The licence of the novelist enables one to put forward readings of character, interpretations of events and so on, which are (or should be) possible, but are not provable; in order to produce a continuous story one must also of course fill in the gaps. But one *must* aim at enlightening the reader rather than obfuscating him; and nothing ever pleases me so much as to hear from a reader (as I often have) that I have caused him or her to seek out the actual sources."

Her ability to reproduce antiquity so faithfully is even more impressive when one realizes that while she knows Latin well, all her Greek is self-taught. She works chiefly from the Loeb Classical Library, a series of Latin and Greek texts interleaved with a translation in English. At St. Hugh's College, Oxford (1924–27), Mary Renault read English; she intended to do a special in Old French but her tutor advised against it because of her difficulties with Anglo-Saxon. Her main historical interest during her undergraduate days was not antiquity at all, but the Middle Ages. Her very first piece of fiction which she consigned to a fiery oblivion after several publishers rejected it was, in her own words, "bred entirely from other people's historical novels with a smattering of Froissart and Malory"—authors who, coincidentally, were the favorites of Elsie Lane in *The Middle Mist* and Ellen Shorland in *North Face*.

It would have seemed more logical to move forward from the Middle Ages instead of backward, but Mary Renault has always done the unexpected. Although she had planned to teach after graduation, she realized that her main interest was writing. Determined to be a novelist and heeding her own conviction that "it would be better to write about real people seen at first hand," she trained as a nurse at Radcliffe Infirmary, Oxford (1933–37) and wrote nothing during that period but a few Christmas skits.

At college, Mary Renault read Plato intermittently, a pastime that continued during her nursing training. Soon she was struck by the drama of the Socratic circle with its wide range of characters. However, she did not yet feel secure enough to attempt a historical novel about the fourth century B.C.; besides, she had an obligation to write about a milieu she knew. With the beginning of World War II, Mary Renault returned to Radcliffe Infirmary as a hospital nurse and remained there until 1945. Her first novel, *Promise of Love*, was published in 1939; it was partly based on her hospital experiences and was so candid that many sisters denied that such things went on in *their* institutions. *Promise of Love* was respectably reviewed; after a successful first novel, she went on to write five more before *The Last of the Wine* established her as the finest interpreter in fiction of ancient Greece.

The Last of the Wine (1956) did not arrive on the literary scene like a spectacularly produced Athena; it was preceded by a long apprenticeship in popular fiction. Few readers are familiar with the author's early work, all of which was a prelude to the Greek novels. Mary Renault is hypercritical of everything she has written before *The Last of the Wine*, except *The Charioteer*. She claims that if her early novels were destroyed irrevocably, she would feel absolutely no loss. Yet these novels were seriously, and often sympathetically, reviewed in such places as the *Times Literary Supple-*

ment, the *New York Times, Saturday Review* (then *Saturday Review of Literature*), *Spectator,* and the *New Yorker.* The significance of the early novels lies in their revelation of the author's discomfort with the present and her veneration of the Hellenic past. These works which are not without literary value are filled with classical allusions and Platonic imagery; for any true evaluation of Mary Renault as an artist, one should observe how she progressed from a contemporary world whose values she measured against antiquity's, to the ancient world whose values were autonomous.

A few technical problems arise in discussing the Greek novels. Because Miss Renault wishes the reader not only to relive the past but also to think in its terms, she does not latinize proper names; in using the classical spellings, she is fulfilling her original purpose of creating as authentic an atmosphere as possible. In his verse translations of the *Iliad* and the *Odyssey,* Robert Fitzgerald also chose to use the classical spellings because they conveyed the sound and euphony of the original. For the reader who has never studied ancient Greek, transliteration can be a *bête noire,* particularly when he finds Alkibiades, Aigeus, and Phoinix for the more familiar Alcibiades, Aegeus, and Phoenix.

Briefly, most Greek proper names have come into English via Latin, and it is customary to replace the Greek letters with their Latin equivalents. Exceptions do exist, especially among certain British and German scholars who still insist upon writing "Aias" for "Ajax." The following table of changes might be useful:

GREEK	LATIN-ENGLISH
ai	ae or e
ei	ī or ē
oi	oe or ē (final oi becomes ī)
ou	ū

u	y
-os	-us
k	c

EXAMPLES: Greek Aischylos = English Aeschylus;
Aristeides = Aristides; Phoibos = Phoebus;
Philippoi = Philippi; Epikouros = Epicurus;
Dionysos = Dionysus; Perikles = Pericles;
Kerkyon = Cercyon; Kroisos = Croesus;
Kallippos = Callippus; Hephaistion = Hephaestion.

Except for direct quotations from the novels, I have chosen to use the more familiar latinized names and to give the classical spelling in a parenthesis the first time the word appears in the discussion—e.g., Chaeronia (Chaironia), Dionysius (Dionysios), Hippolytus (Hippolytos), etc. I have done this for two reasons: first, the latinized spellings are the ones which the reader will invariably recognize; second, should the reader wish to pursue some of the secondary sources Miss Renault recommends, he will usually find that the names have been latinized rather than transliterated.

A good deal of Mary Renault's art lies in her transformation of source material into literature. So that the reader can see how this process is accomplished, I have occasionally juxtaposed a source with a passage from a novel where the historical has been assimilated into the fictive. All translations from the Greek appearing in this study are my own. Since they are designed to convey the thought and not necessarily the style of the original, they are neither literal nor, *triste dictu*, literary.

In preparing this book, I am particularly grateful to former students at Iona College and Fairleigh Dickinson University where I had the opportunity to teach some of Miss Renault's novels in Greek Civilization and Comparative Literature courses; to my wife, a professor of literature and an admirer of Miss Renault's work, who diligently proofread this manuscript; to Professor Peter Wolfe, who wrote the first critical study of the author; and to the novelist herself. This is the second time I have written about a living author. I am continually amazed at how receptive writers are to answering necessary but admittedly trivial questions about their education, dates of attendance at schools, undergraduate literary preferences, influences, and worst of all, interpretations of their own work. Miss Renault was a faithful correspondent; she is also a very learned woman. I have profited as much from some of the interpretations of ancient history she has set forth in her letters as I have from reading her books. Should the Classics ever cease to play a major role in American higher education, it certainly will not be Mary Renault's fault; her fiction which in itself is a course in Greek Civilization mirrors the Horatian ideal that literature should please (*delectare*) and instruct (*docere*). Would that most classicists had been able to achieve a similar mean.

Wherever possible (*Promise of Love* and the Greek novels), I have quoted from paperback editions because of their availability. I would like to express my gratitude to William Morrow & Company, Inc. for permission to quote from *Promise of Love* (Copyright 1939 by Mary Renault), *Kind Are Her Answers* (Copyright 1940 by Mary Renault), *The Middle Mist* (Copyright 1944 by Mary Renault), *Return to Night* (Copyright 1947 by Mary Renault), and *North Face* (Copyright 1948 by Mary Renault); and to Pantheon Books, A Division of Random House, Inc., for permission to quote from *The Charioteer* (Copyright 1953 by Mary Renault), *The Last of the Wine* (Copyright 1956 by Mary Renault), *The King Must Die* (Copyright 1958 by Mary Renault), *The Bull from the Sea* (Copyright 1962 by Mary Renault), *The Mask of Apollo*

(Copyright 1966 by Mary Renault), and *Fire from Heaven* (Copyright 1969 by Mary Renault).

BERNARD F. DICK

Teaneck, New Jersey
January 1972

The Hellenism of Mary Renault

1

The Hospital World

Conrad observed that "every novelist must begin by creating a world, great or little, in which he can honestly believe."[1] The world of Mary Renault's early novels seems microcosmic and dwarfed compared to the Minoan civilization of *The King Must Die* or the Athenian empire of *The Last of the Wine*. Like most novelists, she began by writing about a familiar milieu —the English hospital with its hierarchy of sisters, pathologists, housemen, and surgeons; and its public school morality that drove those who dared (or chose) to flaunt it into a conspiracy of whispers and ellipses. To Mary Renault, whose apprenticeship as a novelist coincided with her years as a nurse during World War II, the sister's uniform, starched and laundered into crisp sterility, mirrors the institution with literal perfection:

> It was a costume which, except for the fact that it could be laundered, bore little reference to physical function which, in fact, it generally hindered. Its purpose was partly that of a religious habit, a reminder of obedience and renunciation; partly, as such habits generally are, a psychic sterilizer, preventing the inconvenient consciousness of personality. In it, all gestures of expression automatically died, leaving only a few of servant-like relaxation, folding the arms, or setting them akimbo.[2]

Promise of Love (1939), known in England as *Purposes of Love*, was Mary Renault's first novel.[3] The hospital provided her with the basic image of a stratified and inflexible society, and it is not surprising that the early novels will reflect a contempt for any environment where canons of conformity are established without regard for human variables. In addition to the doctors and nurses who appeared regularly in her fiction between 1939 and 1953, there are also the "hospital types" whose lives exhibit a similar regimentation and whose ethics are equally monolinear. Included among the misguided who diagnose the unusual as abnormal and the unconventional as immoral are the "faithful" Pedlow of *Kind Are Her Answers*, who would never think that a poison-pen letter would be at variance with her Christian principles; Mrs. Fleming of *Return to Night*, whose warped concept of masculinity caused her son to develop serious doubts about his manhood; and Miss Searle, the virginal don of *North Face*, who viewed any form of romantic behavior with suspicion.

The world of the hospital is essentially that of the matriarchal household, the barracks or the English public school where the unusual or the eccentric are forced to hide behind masks which only a sympathetic eye can penetrate. That such an environment can produce inverts has always been known, and thus homosexuality, whether latent or real, allusive or actual, is a recurrent theme in Mary Renault's fiction. It was only a matter of time before the author's compassion for victims of parochial oppression would lead her to explore the moral standards of ancient Greece where young men like Laurie Odell of *The Charioteer* would never have experienced the isolation of a pariah.

It is difficult to discuss homosexuality in Mary Renault's fiction, for one can be talking about a way of life or a prevailing atmosphere, depending upon the novel in question. In *Promise of Love*, there is no doubt that Colonna Kimball, the nurse with the Grecian hairdo and the Byronic pose, is a lesbian with a typical case history: childhood characterized by parental discord, identification with cowboys in pulp westerns, resentment at the sight of her lover with a man, a stoic resignation to short-lived affairs, spontaneous elation when a patient tells her she reminds him of a male acquaintance. But Colonna is only a minor character; the author's primary concern is a rather unique trio whom she takes through a tangled skein of relationships, overseeing their extrication with an almost Sophoclean sense of dénouement. There is Vivian Lingard, the nurse who can assume a role for every occasion; her brother Jan, one of those charismatic charmers who attracts people of both sexes and then drops them like "unfinished symphonies"; and his close friend, Mic Freeborn, an assistant pathologist, whose unusual behavior is explained in the customary ellipsis, " 'When you meet Mic . . . be easy on him. . . . He's had a very—' " (p. 14).

Mary Renault's method of characterization in her early fiction consisted of a suggestive naturalism which explained human actions in terms of family influences, the hastily formed judgments of others, and, of course, the regimentation of the hospital world. Sometimes the sympathetic nurse would overcome the talented novelist, and she would resort to a casebook approach where details of a character's early environment would appear at odd points in the novel like so much testimony on his behalf. Colonna Kimball even describes herself as "a rather humdrum psycopathic case, conforming to the textbooks" (p. 273). On the other hand, Mic Freeborn is neither a case nor a homosexual, although he does produce a picture of his school friend, Colin, when Vivian asks if he had any lovers before her. Mic was simply a victim of one of those "special friendships" for which English public schools (and American private ones) are notorious.

It is nurse Vivian Lingard who is the most complex figure in the novel. The parochialism of the hospital world requires the donning of a mask; Vivian's, like that of most Renault characters, acquired its impenetrability in a bipolar childhood—actress mother vs. scholar father. To Vivian, the personality is a stage where "there ought to be a green-room and a looking-glass at which to remove make-up and change it for the next act" (p. 29). She tosses aside remarks "with the hurried naturalness of an actor concealing a muffed cue" (p. 37), and justifies her facade by claiming that it shows one's aims, although not necessarily one's achievements.

Vivian's repertoire comprises three basic roles (nurse, lover, intellectual), each of which is flexible enough to admit of variations for the occasion (nurse-goddess, bitch-lover, dilettante-intellectual). She allows herself to be fondled by Colonna for the same reason, as she muses, that it would be boorish not to offer a Siamese cat a saucer of milk. Yet Vivian's femininity is never questioned; she is not only the eternal female but also the Earth Mother who can accommodate lesbians like Colonna, young men in search of their manhood like Mic, and dashing lechers like Scot-Hallard. When Colonna becomes aware of the aura that envelops Vivian, she loses all interest in the physical. The two lie in still repose like figures on a Grecian urn:

> The night had grown windy, and the stars seemed to be cruising at speed between lazily drifting wreaths of cloud. They lay side by side and watched; the rhythm was hypnotic and lovely, spinning round them a thickening web of silence. Colonna's drowsy weight and faint fragrance were companionable and undemanding. [P. 28]

The description is sensual but unerotic, and its Hellenic simplicity evokes a lost pastoral world; one thinks of a Theocritean idyll where two shepherds find a sexless quiescence in each other's song. Thus to inquire whether or not a homosexual act ever transpired between Colonna and Vivian is as ludicrous and naïve as asking whether Achilles and Patroclus were lovers. The traditional classroom answer has always been, "Probably, but not in the *Iliad*," and one might give the same reply to those who have found more in Mary Renault's characters than she had chosen to disclose.

What is significant about *Promise of Love* is not the existence of a dubious sexuality which is a *donnée*, but rather the treatment of the subject. A first novel often manifests the beginnings of an author's future techniques and preoccupations, themes and counterthemes, characters who will recur under various names, and attitudes that will be altered but never transformed. *Promise of Love* is such a novel, and contained within it are the indictment of a monolinear society; a homosexual atmosphere that is sometimes only as superficial as the epicene repartee in Plato's *Lysis* or *Symposium*; the sympathetic treatment of the sensitive youth with a bruised masculine ego; lovemaking described metaphorically by falling petals and typographically by the dash and the ellipsis; the world as theatre; and above all, the attempt to create some sort of Hellenic referent with ubiquitous allusions to Greek history and mythology (Alcibiades, Socrates, Persephone, Thetis, Hera) which should, but do not always, form a skeleton on which the flesh of the novel hangs.

The allusiveness with which love, particularly *l'amour qui n'ose pas dire son nom*, is handled is reminiscent of the *Lysis* where an undercurrent of mock homosexual wit is present but never allowed to overwhelm the more important topics of friendship and the good. Thus Socrates is completely sympathetic when Hippothales speaks of his inability to capture the boy Lysis for himself. In fact, Socrates even goes so far as to show him how the courting should be done. When Socrates greets Lysis, the atmosphere is charged with sparks of sexually ambiguous wit which a good many classical scholars overlook or simply enjoy without communicating their pleasure to anyone.

In *Promise of Love* there is a similar atmosphere of *entre nous* quips and double entendres that suggest ultra sophistication; however, they have as little to do with the theme of the novel as the intimations of pederasty have to do with the definition of friendship in the *Lysis*. When Vivian stands outside the door of Mic's flat, he casually says, " 'Push it, my dear, it isn't locked' " (p. 20), thinking it was her brother Jan. The sight of Plato's *Symposium* elicits a remark from Vivian about the sins of the Greeks. She responds to Mic's disclosure of his illegitimacy with a "My dear" in a tone that one woman uses to another. Their first kiss causes Vivian to play the sullied virgin, and when Mic challenges the pose, she retorts with " 'I'm sorry . . . to upset you. I forgot you're not accustomed to women' " (p. 70). Allusions to Marlowe's *Edward II*, statements like "Socrates had the right idea," references to Oscar Wilde's green carnation, and comments about Alcibiades and the public school mores complete the picture of moral emancipation in the late 1930s.

More important than the sexual ambiguity of *Promise of Love* is the tenuous network of Greek allusions and ideals that is loosely worked throughout the novel. In all her early fiction, with the possible exception of *Kind Are Her Answers*, Mary Renault is demanding that the reader view her characters with a double vision and consider them as Hellenic souls imprisoned in modern bodies. An identification with Greek prototypes and ideals may seem hopelessly naïve and even impractical today; since *Ulysses*, all mythic fiction seems anachronistic. But the reviewers who hailed Mary Renault's early novels as works of considerable depth never found the allusive undercurrents that ran beneath the narrative line like a secret spring for the educated.

Consider the depiction of Vivian's look-alike brother, Jan Lingard. That he transcends sexuality is clear from Vivian's description of him as an enigmatic man with a "somewhat remote and disquieting smile often found on the statuary of archaic Greece" (p. 11). When Jan reenters the plot as an ill-starred *deus ex machina* to extricate his sister from her romantic entanglements, he realizes that he too must play a role in an action that is moving from popular fiction to the Sophoclean cosmos:

> There came upon him slowly a sense, not of shame which was an emotion out of his sphere, but of indemnity, of being concerned in atonement; the kind of guilt in which the Greeks believed. . . . The assent, he thought, was all. Life was not so lacking in design that an occasion of symmetry would be refused him. Already it was waiting, contained in the present as these black branches contained next summer's leaves. [Pp. 242–43]

In this fatalistic acquiescence which foreshadows "the consenting" of Theseus in *The King Must Die,* Jan becomes a scapegoat whose death will occur during his errand of mercy.

Vivian is also a mythic creation. She revels in role-playing, and her favorite part is the ethereal divinity who lavishes her favors on mortals. When she gives herself to Mic, she feels "infinite, ancient in wisdom, protective as Hera, a mother of gods and men" (p. 113). Then with Mic's disclosure that his first lover was a male, she turns to another role—the Homeric Hera who taunts and belittles her mate. Mic is infuriated when

Vivian dons men's clothes, and the situation is hardly remedied by her offer to serve him like Ganymede. With the surgeon Scot-Hallard, it will be a different role—the mysterious Persephone who will visit the daylight world before returning to the shadows of twilight with Mic.

Vivian is also caught in that peculiarly Greek vice which Socrates is always criticizing—ignorance of how to achieve one's excellence or *arete*. Mary Renault frequently uses the word "excellence," and it is always with a Platonic connotation. When Vivian realizes "the gulf that still separated her from simple adequacy in her work, still less from any kind of excellence" (p. 50), "excellence" is used in the Greek sense of *arete*, a highly complex word that means, among other things, being good at one's craft.[4] Vivian has not achieved her excellence in nursing, a profession into which she drifted in the perennial quest for identity. Nor has she achieved it in the intellectual sphere, for although her literary interests set her apart from the other nurses, she can only speak in quotations and make cryptic generalizations about the Greeks.

In the last two chapters Vivian and Mic achieve their *arete*, but in another sense of this remarkable word—self-knowledge as well as professional perfection. Their self-knowledge, however, was attained only through the death of Jan, and the love they find at the end of the novel is a sober, asexual kind founded on the death of another. In the last chapters, the author allows each of them to experience the consequences of a sacrificial offering.[5]

Vivian realizes that henceforth she will be the lover, and Mic the beloved. Her playacting has ended, and with the final curtain has come the end of her divinity. She is no longer Persephone, nor Hera, mother of gods and men, but simply a woman who "like water . . . had found her own level" (p. 309). Mic has acquired a similar form of knowledge; he too has found his *arete* which, professionally, will mean assuming the head of a cancer hospital. For Mic the beloved, it will also mean an understanding of the lover, "her knowledge and tenderness, her moods which, lacking the strength to control them, she had imagination enough to criticize and invest with an individual grace" (p. 312).

Although the final passages seem to rise to a Platonic mysticism that lacerates the syntax, the basic meaning is clear. As Mic reads Malory to Vivian by the hearth, the lovers bask in a passionless glow; when he kisses her, he feels "the reasonless, cosmic pity that troubles love when it is loosened from passion" (p. 313). The scene is not quite as asexual as the end of *Strange Interlude* where Nina and Charlie are enveloped in the golden haze of impotence, but it does suggest the quiescence that comes once passion is spent. The scene also suggests the ultimate stage of Platonic love, mutual affection (*philia*), and the tableau of Vivian asleep at Mic's side recalls the true lover of the *Phaedrus* who is willing to sleep like a servant at the side of his beloved.

None of the reviewers noticed the sunken Platonic imagery in *Promise of Love*, yet it was the Socratic *arete* and the theory of love expressed in the *Phaedrus* that raised the novel above the level of a romance with a hospital setting. In her second novel, *Kind Are Her Answers* (1940), Mary Renault was dealing with even more conventional material—a doctor approaching thirty and in dire need of an extramarital affair which he succeeds in having with a rather vapid nymph who thinks that the *Sunflowers* was painted by somebody called Gogh.

To a doctor like Kit Anderson who prefers the shadows of London anonymity to the mild spotlight which small towns turn on their local celebrities, there is little difference between hospital parochialism and rural provincialism, especially when he decides to dabble in adultery with the relative of an old patient. The setting is again the Cotswolds, and Mary Renault also tries to merge, but without her initial success, the two worlds—hospital and theatre, real and illusory—into a planet-satellite relationship. Unfortunately, the music of the spheres is never heard, and the author's theory of society as a microcosmic theatre where amateurs and professionals interact is lost in a *ménage à trois* that reads like superior magazine fiction.

There are the usual innuendoes about sex and virility. Kit asks his wife Janet if she had a crush on a school friend and justifies his query with " 'We're all products of the system.' " [6] This is the kind of dialogue that would have been meaningful in *Promise of Love*, but here it is merely floating in a contextual vacuum. Young Timmie Curtis, a nineteen-year-old Oxford Grouper who develops a crush on Janet, is a blurred carbon of the Renault youth in search of his manhood. In describing his interest in the Group, he censors his language of anything that might be less than manly: " 'Of course we all thought religion was siss—pretty soft' " (p. 80). And the episode in which he informs Kit, man to man, that he is in love with Janet again shows the compassion the author has for the young who must continually prove themselves.

Kind Are Her Answers is one of those novels that implies more than it actually states. It is reminiscent of an undergraduate essay filled with brilliant ideas which tease the imagination but which also remain tantalizing intimations of what might have been. The world is again a stage, and Christie Heath, the young actress with whom Kit has an affair and who will presumably become his second wife (barring World War II), projects her own theatricality into her relationships with men.

She and Kit literally play the backstreet lovers with their own code for posting letters and phoning each other. When Kit agrees to act at the Brimpton Abbey Theater merely to be near his mistress, his audition is embarrassingly amateurish and symbolizes his inability to playact successfully in life. Kit cannot lead "that curious double life in which one was both the trick and the effect" (p. 267).

Mary Renault devotes a considerable amount of space (pp. 209–13) to describing a biblical pageant at the Abbey. She omits no details, including the audience's awed murmur at the Annunciation tableau and an angel's collision with the Madonna. She also provides her own running commentary on the performance, criticizing the actress playing Gabriel for being too feminine and lauding Christie's interpretation of the Madonna with a qualifying statement that she would have been completely out of place as a Mater Dolorosa. The episode itself is unimportant, but it does indicate the author's penchant for stage description which will be seen to better effect in *The Mask of Apollo* and *Fire from Heaven* where she actually stages Euripides' *Bacchae* from the points of view of the actor, spectator, and playwright.

There is one incident in *Kind Are Her Answers* which might be used to illustrate what happens when a scenario is disguised as a novel. During an argument Kit bundles Christie into his car; their conversation spans a whole page, and then one suddenly reads: " 'Well, we need something,' said Kit taking a sandwich (they were having tea in Paxton), 'living the way we do' " (p. 234).

A swift change of scene is hardly unusual in literature. Yet this intruding parenthesis, acceptable in an acting edition of a play or in a scenario, somehow throws the problem of the novel into high relief: it is an eternal triangle film script written by someone who has too much talent for her present task and who therefore fills in the hollow spaces with some intriguing ideas on life as a stage and religion as therapy. Yet this is the same Mary Renault who in *The King Must Die* permanently captured the magnificence of the Gulf of Corinth for the tourists who could never articulate their impressions.

The art of word-painting is not achieved overnight, and those who were awed by her Grecian landscapes might consider a description of an autumn scene in the Cotswolds in this minor novel:

> They entered the camp through a gap in the wall, the ancient gate, perhaps, of the citadel. Within, the bowl-shaped circle of the wood was filled to the brim with broken light. The sun on its downward course struck through open places between the half-stripped trees, and gave everything it touched the glow of metal without its hardness or its cold. It moulded itself in plaques to the tree trunks, and lay strewn in softly shifting flakes on the ground. Leaves in its path were turned golden transparencies, so clear that it would not have been hard to believe one saw the visible movement of sap through the veins. Only in the western rim of the hollow a thin crescent of shadow was beginning. [P. 145]

Such art seems curiously out of place in a *ménage à trois*, almost like a Poussin carefully hung in a railway station.

In her review of *Kind Are Her Answers*, Rosamond Lehmann prophesied: "Mary Renault is, I feel, at a dangerous cross-roads in her career. Popular she will be. It is to be hoped that nothing and no one will persuade her to pour herself out in an unstemmed flow of fiction during the next few years." [7] With a four-year hiatus between her second and third novels, one is almost tempted to think that the author heeded her reviewer's advice, but it was really the Second World War and her return to nursing that temporarily checked the flow of fiction.

Like *Purposes of Love* which underwent a title change in the United States, *The Friendly Young Ladies* (1944) became *The Middle Mist* (1945) for American readers, much to Mary Renault's annoyance. The new title came from a Rupert Brooke sonnet, part of which also formed the epigraph. The title was so unconventionally alliterative that Russell Maloney, the critic for the *New Yorker*, could not take it seriously. Yet it was his review, alternately glib and contradictory, that conveyed the mixed feelings most readers had toward the book. The novel was a "tidbit," "capably written," and the kind of fiction "we used to get in tins from Fortnum & Mason before the war." Although "we would once have considered this a superior novel . . . even now it's undeniably charming." [8]

"Charming" was hardly the right word for this tale of "wanderers in the middle mist," but it was indicative of an attitude a magazine critic might take toward a love story that was a disguised Platonic tract. Somehow a noncommittal adjective can absolve a reviewer from coming to grips with Plato's elusive vocabulary ("friend," "companion," "enemy"), not to mention the enigmatic passage from the *Lysis* that appears at the end.

Like *Promise of Love*, the ending of *The Middle Mist* should also be read in terms of Platonism, primarily the philosophy of the *Lysis*, an intriguing dialogue in which the subject of friendship is discussed, at times with a tortuous literalism, but never really defined. In one sense, the Rupert Brooke poem, a memorial to those trapped between love's extremes of ecstasy and anguish ("Who cry for shadows, clutch, and cannot tell/

Whether they love at all, or loving, whom") ironically sums up the novel; for *The Middle Mist*, written with an art that by present standards is more quaint than compelling, vacillates between being a philosophical treatise and a case history in much the same way as its characters waver between friendship and eros.

A case study of the Lane family is provided at the outset. There is the father who yearned for a son in compensation for his two daughters; the mother who also wanted a son but primarily to protect her from her husband's insults; the younger daughter, Elsie, who reverted to a medieval fantasy world of Malory and Tennyson; and the older daughter, Leonora ("Leo"), who left home at nineteen with a dramatic declaration of independence: " 'If I were a man I wouldn't be here. And I bloody well wish I were.' " [9]

When Elsie goes in search of her sister whom she had not seen in eight years, she discovers that Leo is living with another woman, Helen Vaughn, on a houseboat in the Thames. The recognition scene is done with great skill and an almost perverse deftness. It is also one of the few times that the author is consistent in her use of point of view, for the reader witnesses the reunion through the eyes of a teenager who prides herself on being "seventeen-and-a-half years old."

Elsie is waiting in a pub for a ferry to take her to the houseboat. In the pub are a fair-haired girl who is playing darts, and a slender "boy" with effeminately long hair. When the boy turned around, "in one moment there fell from Elsie not only the events of the day, but those of the last eight years. For a glance was enough to show her that Leo had hardly changed at all" (p. 54). It is even more significant that after Leo walks away from the bar, the conversation of the men continued "without the change of key which is usually observable when the last of the female element leaves."

Leo and Helen have been accepted, and there is no reason why they should not be; they are, as old Mr. Hicks observes, " 'a couple of real nice, friendly young ladies.' "

The Middle Mist was inspired by Radclyffe Hall's *The Well of Loneliness* (1928), a novel about lesbianism which only Havelock Ellis seems to have admired as literature. The book traced the heroine's neurosis to her christening where she received the name of Stephen because her parents were expecting a boy. When Mary Renault reached the episode where Mary Llewellyn saw Stephen's "heavy silk masculine underwear," she went into a convulsion of laughter which resulted in *The Middle Mist*, a much more sophisticated treatment of women in love.

The atmosphere seems to be suggestively lesbianic, and there are times when currents of sexual ambiguity appear to be circulating in *The Middle Mist*. Of all the reviews, Henry Reed's was the most astute and delicately phrased; he felt that the characters have "pasts which are left too much to conjecture for their pressure on the present to be comprehensible to the reader." [10] But the fact that Mary Renault decided not to transform the evocative into the factual may mean either that she chose to think of Leo as a tomboy in her mid-twenties (as did some of the critics) or that Leo's playing Huckleberry Finn indicated more of a disinterest in sex than a tendency toward lesbianism. For some reason, the more aloof from the erotic a character is, the more open he becomes to imputations of homosexuality. Even Euripides' Hippolytus and Waugh's Sebastian Flyte have not escaped criticism by the knowledgeable. Kate O'Brien's complaint, "I could not make out what was up with Leonora," [11] is well taken, but her review should have made some reference to the ending where it is quite clear that "what was up with Leonora" was simply her desire to have a nonphysical relationship with men, and

one would also assume, with women. Reading anything more into the houseboat *ménage* would be tanta-
mount to committing the heresy of psychology (which,
critically, is as censorable as the heresy of paraphrase)
and using the findings of a discipline that is "unnecessary
to art and not in itself of artistic value." [12]

In *Promise of Love*, Mic Freeborn wrote a letter to
Vivian in which he characterized both of them as be-
longing to their sexes "rather incidentally" (p. 74); the
same can be said of Leo, Helen, and Joe Flint, their
author-friend, in *The Middle Mist*. Actually, the relationship between Leo and Helen is so sexually antiseptic
that it precludes the possibility of the physical. It is true
that Helen at first regards Elsie as an intruder, but little
is made of her resentment. It is simply *there*, and one
can easily overreact to it. Moreover, both women are
involved in their own professional activities (Helen il-
lustrates medical textbooks, and Leo writes westerns
under a man's pseudonym), and in their conversations
they are by no means loath to discuss men.

One imagines that *The Middle Mist* was to have been
an elaborately conceived novel, a work in which the
surface behavior of the characters would clash with their
true selves and where points of view would grow con-
centrically out of each other. In a sense, Mary Renault
has written a prolegomenon to such a novel. The surface
is extremely well defined, for it is one where the ellipses
are more significant than completed sentences. However,
the author has covered herself against the charge of
superficiality. When Elsie picks up a copy of Joe's novel,
she realizes with the accurate but halting uncertainty
of an adolescent that "one was living on a brittle surface,
and that underneath it things might be other than what
they seemed" (p. 119).

But it is only a surface and remains such because the
characters, despite their checkered pasts, are really

innocents who feel more intensely than they reason. To Elsie, the houseboat is the adult world where emancipated women drink, smoke, make sly remarks about men, and sing bawdy songs. To Dr. Peter Bracknell, the houseboat represents an environment that is not completely natural, although he is unable to articulate his feelings about it. The quizzical wonder he manifests is that of the bourgeois who is exposed to an iconoclastic society for the first time and confuses its amorality with immorality. Peter is the kind of male who measures women by a sexual criterion that is inapplicable to Helen and Leo, who belong to their sexes "rather incidentally." He congratulates Leo on being "normally sexed" (as if the opposite would be a fate worse than death) and with an almost laughable compassion remarks that her relationship with Helen " 'must demand great courage . . . from both of you' " (p. 220).

In her early fiction, Mary Renault was criticized for her handling of multiple point of view, a factor which might partially explain the lack of clarity in the emotional relationships between characters in *The Middle Mist*. Initially, Elsie Lane was the focal character, and the reader viewed a mildly "naughty" adult world with its bohemian types and their sexual emancipation through the eyes of an innocent abroad. But by the middle of the novel, the emphasis has shifted to Leo and Joe, who complement each other in much the same way as a hack writer would be attracted to a creative novelist; or, on a more pragmatic level, as a writer of westerns who never set foot in America would gravitate to a native Arizonan. The novel then begins to revolve around an illusion-truth, artifice-reality axis; still it must have some core, some referent to which everything else is subordinate. A mature viewpoint is required to give the book some sort of artistic rationale. There is just so much one can see through a teenager's limited vision.

Toward the end of *The Middle Mist*, another point of view begins to emerge; it is the omniscient author's, or rather the omniscient author's attempt to cast Leo and Joe as lovers on the verge of tragic awareness. It is only then that one realizes that the novel is really about Leo, who, far from being lesbianic, has actually achieved a state of sexual transcendence by denying the accidents of her femininity and keeping its essence intact. Thus her penchant for wearing men's clothes and for decorating her bedroom with cowboy pictures in no way militates against her womanhood which goes beyond anything society has deemed feminine. Like Vivian Lingard, Leo is playing the part of a goddess; her body will relinquish its divinity in the act of love and will take on a humanity that brings with it the pain of self-knowledge.

Those who objected to the final chapter of *Promise of Love* might raise similar objections to the Platonism at the end of *The Middle Mist* where there is a twofold recognition: Joe's discovery of the "two persons" in Leo, and Leo's realization that love embodies a necessary element of evil or imperfection. In his letter to Leo, Joe distinguished between the friend whose companionship he cherished and the woman whose body he possessed:

> There are two people in you. One of them I have known much longer than the other. I am missing him, already, as much as I ever missed a friend. . . . To the friend and companion I had, if his integrity comes first of all, I am worse than useless now, I am an enemy. [P. 276]

Explicating the letter with its Platonic vocabulary is almost as grammatically precarious as discussing the "we of me" in *The Member of the Wedding*. To Joe, Leo the friend was a "he"; the Greeks would have said *hetairos*, a male companion, someone familiar and trusted, and to Socrates a *hetairos* was more valuable than any other possession. But Joe has lost this companion and friend through the proverbial *nuit d'amour*, and what was to have been a relationship that went beyond sex disintegrated into a physical act that shattered the idealism of lover and beloved.

In Plato's *Symposium*, Pausanias distinguished two kinds of Eros: physical infatuation caused by the Common Aphrodite; and the nobler type, engendered by the Heavenly Aphrodite, whose only purpose is the spiritual perfection of the beloved in an act of friendship. The intrusion of physical desire destroyed the Platonic bond which united Joe and Leo; the loss of the stable affection (*philia*) which they once had produces the sadness and uncertainty that come with any fall from innocence. Joe has become the enemy of his beloved, and after reading the letter, Leo rushes to Plato's *Lysis* and turns to a familiar passage:

> For these things are called friends for the sake of a friend, but our true friend seems to be of a nature exactly the reverse of this; for it was found to be our friend for the sake of an enemy; but, if the enemy were removed, no longer, it seems, do we possess a friend. [P. 274]

Anyone who ever studied Greek would sense the ruthless literalism of the translation, and the Greekless reader would be appalled, and rightly so, at the inelegant English. Yet the passage holds great meaning for Leo, but apparently not for the reviewers who blithely ignored what is undoubtedly the key to a highly enigmatic novel.

Leo could not have selected a more inconclusive dialogue or a more puzzling passage if she tried. The *Lysis* probably belongs to Plato's "Socratic Period," and is therefore characterized by the lack of a conclusion. It is a dialogue about friendship, specifically its definition.

The excerpt in question (*Lysis* 220E) occurs in the third stage of the quest for a definition. First Socrates explored the range of possible meanings in the word *philos* —friend, lover, beloved. But who is our *philos*? Is it someone we love? Suppose that the love is not returned, for is it not true that we can be friends of our enemies and enemies of our friends? Or is friendship predicated on the old idea of "like is friend to like"? The good therefore love the good, and the evil love the evil. Yet friendship is based on longing, but we do not long for what is like us, but rather for our opposite. But if this is true, then just men would love the unjust.

Socrates' abandoning of the "like is friend to like" position leads into Leo's favorite passage which should be read in the light of the true Platonic lover. To Plato, love itself is neither good nor evil, and the lover is also midway between the two extremes. Since he is neither good nor bad, wise nor ignorant, he yearns to possess goodness and wisdom. He loves because there is some "evil" present. If evil is regarded as ignorance or imperfection, the picture becomes clearer. The lover does not really know the good; if he did, he would not desire it. One only yearns for what one lacks. Love then embodies an element of evil; call it ignorance, imperfection, or desire. It is the presence of evil that makes us love the good just as it is the existence of disease that makes the body love health.

If the enemy were removed, no longer, it seems, do we possess a friend. Substitute "desire" for "enemy," and the argument is clear: Remove passion from love, and there is no love. Yet desire (*epithumia*) which is non-physical and morally neutral is not to be confused with *eros*, as a passage from the *Phaedrus* (223D) makes quite clear: "If you think that friendship cannot be strong without passion, you must remember that then we could not hold our sons dear, nor our fathers and mothers; nor could we possess trustworthy friends whom we acquired not through passion but through pursuits of a different kind."

Desire of the nonconsummated kind is necessary for friendship, but the passion engendered by the Common Aphrodite would be a barrier to it. By putting his relationship with Leo on an erotic plane, Joe became an "enemy" to his friend. And his friend and companion now realizes that a necessary component of *philia*, the striving toward what one does not yet possess (the good), has been lost.

These are extremely complex ideas—too complex for popular fiction on the one hand, and too profound for Joe and Leo on the other. It is really Mary Renault who is projecting this form of self-knowledge into them, for it is impossible to believe that Joe, with all his learning, knew he was speaking like a member of Socrates' circle who lost his boy-companion; and it is equally difficult to think that Leo, a writer of cowboy novels, could fully understand what she had read in the *Lysis*.[13]

According to Leo's simplified Platonism, what was lost was not only innocence but a Hellenic dreamworld where she could have been treated like an equal, like "a man with his friend, emotion-free, objective, concerned not with relationships but with work and things, sharing ideas" (p. 166).

When she reflects that only with Joe could she have had "the company of her kind . . . without the destuctive bias of sexual attraction or rejection," she is really echoing Plato's views on sex. Despite what has been said about Plato's morals, it is clear from the *Dialogues* that he despised homosexuality as much as heterosexuality. "What he disliked was sexual relations of any kind." [14]

Despite all the tragic implications of a lost Platonism, Mary Renault manages to suggest that once Leo has been demythologized (or deplatonized), she is ready for true love. This, one presumes, is a sop for the female readers who like their women characters unphilosophical and lachrymose. It is fitting that the novel which began with Elsie's entering the parlor of her bickering parents should end with Peter Bracknell's tapping at Leo's window and rehearsing what he would say when they meet again. He is unaware of Leo's newly acquired (but under the circumstances, useless) humanity, nor does he see that she is weeping the tears of a woman.

An excerpt from a Laurence Binyon poem provided both the title and the epigraph for Mary Renault's fourth novel, *Return to Night* (1947). Like the poem and its "leaves of lovely gloom," the novel is bathed in a crepuscular light. After reading it, one is convinced that a few chapters must have taken place in daytime, but somehow there is only the memory of shadowy caves, coffee at the fireplace, a confession of family secrets at sunset, and an ever-present aura of sadness which twilight often brings.

Set in the Cotswolds on the eve of World War II, *Return to Night* revives the hospital milieu of *Promise of Love*—the provincial setting that requires the unconventional to be masked at all times; the female surgeon who plays the role of the emancipated woman; the youth who turns to the theatre because of his inferiority as a male; and his puritanical mother who caused his self-doubts by her inability to distinguish between good looks and effeminacy.

Hilary Mansell, who describes herself as a second-rate surgeon, is a typical Renault poseur, just as her lover, Julian Fleming, is the familiar youth who gives every indication of being a homosexual except the most obvious one. Certainly his bedside manner with Hilary is so casually masculine that any reader with suspicions will be forced to rethink the entire characterization. This ambiguity is intentional, and the fact that it is so pervasive is due to the author's emphatic belief that a sensitivity slightly tinged by the effete is not necessarily synonymous with homosexuality. The mercurial youth who casually tosses off a "My dear" is light-years removed from the homosexual who inflects with a vengeance ("My *dear!*"). The italics and the punctuation make all the difference.

All one can say with certainty about Julian Fleming is that he is essentially a male whose mother-dominated childhood has given him some of the mannerisms of the female. When he disparages the fastidiousness of women, his intonation "suggested, irresistibly, aunts, school matrons and nagging devoted maids." [15] When Julian was a child, his mother apologized for his fascination with his aunt's makeup by claiming that he was really quite a manly little chap. To Mrs. Fleming, Julian grew up under the "handicap" of being extremely good-looking; she was also convinced that he was born into the wrong sex: " 'You should have been a woman; I've wished, often, that you had been one' " (p. 377). Under the circumstances it is amazing that Julian could be so proficient at making love to Hilary. In her own unobtrusive way, Mary Renault indicates Julian's masculine side by describing the naturalness of his first night with Hilary, who discovered in his bureau drawer a marriage manual and an RAF brochure.

Julian's attraction to the theatre would be inevitable. His lack of confidence in his masculinity would rule out romantic leads, or at least on the stage. Yet when he and Hilary are in a dark cave, Julian recites Romeo's final speech to her. He brings an air of theatricality even to his courtship of an older woman; there is something ironic and even poignant about Julian's playing a role in a cave which he could never enact in a theater. He prefers character roles of the otherworldly type (Oberon and Caliban) and revels in the elaborate masklike makeup which the parts require. It is understandable that he would wish to conceal a face which his mother constantly reminded him was too handsome.

There is a delicacy about the exposition in *Return to Night* which suggests a world where secrets are strung together like the loops and circles of a lace tablecloth. It is to the author's credit that she drops allusions to Julian's childhood at random in the novel, and the missing pieces are supplied in the penultimate chapter where Mrs. Fleming discloses that her first husband was an actor, a bigamist, and presumably Julian's real father whose "weaknesses" (good looks and a flair for the stage) their son apparently inherited.

Julian is one of Mary Renault's Greeks taken out of his Hellenic environment and thrown into an alien world. Lying on his hospital bed, "he looked like the flower of Sparta brought back from Thermopylae on a shield" (p. 22). When Hilary first sees him on horseback, he resembles a timeless *objet d'art* of stone or bronze. They come into a cave as if they were entering the mouth of Tartarus. Julian's interpretation of Shakespeare's Oberon embodies qualities of Euripides' Dionysus in the *Bacchae*. When Hilary sees Julian by lamplight, he is Eros to her Psyche; when he comes in out of the rain, he is Leander to her Hero.

At the close of the novel they are back in the cave. Julian and Hilary have undergone a *rite de passage*, and in almost cinematic fashion they freeze into figures of myth. She becomes Demeter, and he the symbolic grain which must be allowed to grow unimpeded. The ending is inconclusive, but any love story set in 1938 could only have a hypothetically happy ending, if one at all.

Return to Night was generally well regarded, and it is this novel which, in addition to winning the MGM award,[16] also acquired for the author the most flattering blurb a novelist could receive: "an artist to her finger-tips." [17] There were some objections to Julian's being a "case" and to a one-sided point of view which made the reader see everything through Hilary's eyes, but the general consensus was that in less skilled hands the love story of a woman of thirty-four and a young man eleven years her junior would merely have been mawkish.

Looking at the novel in retrospect, one is struck by the tastefulness and lyricism with which the love affair is handled. Somehow it is all terribly quaint today. Julian comes to Hilary's bed, his face transfigured by moonlight. Hilary becomes a goddess in some eternal fertility rite in which she will enact an Earth Mother yielding her divinity to a mortal. The prose is sensual, and it has always been characteristic of Mary Renault that while she dealt with the most personal of human emotions, she either suggested metaphors for them or else used a cinematic approach where the author's omniscient eye, like the camera lens, moved away from the recumbent lovers, leaving them to their solitude:

> As she bent to him, and saw his face, white and transformed in the moonlight, flung back in an un-breathing stillness for her kiss, she felt the weight of magic and of legend thrown on her so heavily that she dared not speak. . . . She felt as though it were taking the soul from her own, and was afraid; but the power of the dream held her silent; she could only comfort him in her arms, while, rapt and trembling, he contended with his mystery. It was as if in the kiss she had entered it with him; as if she became, even to herself, an ageless source, a shelter and a benediction. [P. 252]

One can now understand why the publishers objected to the novel's original title, *The Sacred River*; they assumed the public would think it was about the Ganges.

North Face (1948) was also in the *amor omnia vincit* tradition: an embittered schoolmaster suffering from postwar malaise and an unfortunate marriage meets, romances, and finally marries a young secretary with an almost incestuous devotion to the memory of her childhood sweetheart. Yet it is unfair to say the author has written a woman's novel, for although her early work will always be classified as popular fiction, *North Face*, more than any of the others, reveals Mary Renault's triumph over her drearily sentimental material.

The setting is a seaside guest house called Wier View, and the time is shortly after World War II. The resort is practically a hospital, for it has the antiquated gentility of a "spinster sitting in a disproportionately high-backed chair" [18]—a description that recalls the nurses' chairs in *Promise of Love* which could only have been designed for "straight-backed Victorian children." There are also the "hospital types"—an unmarried female don (Miss Searle) who is not beyond reporting any embrace that seems to verge on fornication; a sensible nurse (Miss Fisher) to whom sex is a fact of life; and the spiritually wounded lovers, Neil Langton and Ellen Shorland.

Again it is Mary Renault's style that raises the novel above the level of magazine fiction. The two spinsters at Wier View, Miss Searle and Miss Fisher, the professional virgin and the professional career woman respectively, are delineated by their actions, their attitudes toward literature, and in one of the author's most incisive descriptions, by the momentary union of their hands as each reaches down to retrieve a ball of wool:

> For a moment their hands met on the ball: the hand of the scholar, meticulous, with fineness but no strength in the bone, taut veins blue under the thin skin at the back, the nails ribbed, brittle and flecked here and there with white; the other broad-palmed

and short-fingered, with aggressive smooth cleanliness that comes of much scrubbing with antiseptic followed by much compensating cream, the nails filed short and round, their holiday varnish spruce. [P. 8]

Despite its attempt to deal realistically with loneliness and passion, *North Face* is a literary novel where everyone has an opinion on everything from Plato's *Crito* to *No Orchids for Miss Blandish*. Miss Fisher dimly recalls *The Canterbury Tales* as a "thin feuilleton," and her attempt to read "The Miller's Tale" sends her thumbing incredulously through the glossary. Miss Searle is always quoting Ovid or Shakespeare, and Neil, the classicist, has a penchant for the *Aeneid*.

Most of the time the literary allusions do nothing but form a chain of decorative *obiter dicta*; but in one instance a literary reference is expertly used as a means of characterization. Miss Fisher, who lost an educated beau by confusing Housman with "houseman," turns to her companion, and in an action prompted by genuine curiosity and middle-aged loneliness, asks her to read a passage from Chaucer. Miss Searle, always the teacher, accepts the challenge of *vulgarisation* and selects the *Balade de Bon Conseil* which she reads with a slight concession to modern pronunciation.

In another instance, the author tries, but without complete success, to suggest parallels between the emotional responses of her characters and Vergil's. That a Classics teacher should quote Vergil is understandable; but the Classics teacher is Neil Langton, whose wife's infidelity indirectly caused the death of their daughter. Moreover, the passage he recalls is from the *Aeneid* (4. 522–23) where the tranquillity of nature stands in marked contrast to the sleeplessness of the ill-starred Dido.

The allusion to Dido recurs when Miss Searle, whose mind is always fermenting with literary references before bedtime, reflects on moonlight, a shore, and a discarded sword. She finally concludes her literary solitaire by quoting a verse from the passage in *The Merchant of Venice* (5.1) where Lorenzo describes Dido with a willow in her hand, bidding farewell to Aeneas.

Mary Renault seemed to be trying to superimpose the Dido-Aeneas legend on *North Face*, which is not even remotely a mythic novel. It is true that Ellen is as fanatically devoted to the memory of her beloved Jock as Dido was to Sychaeus, and one cannot deny that Neil possesses Aeneas' postwar weariness. Perhaps the evening they spent in the lane was supposed to evoke the cave episode of *Aeneid* 4. Still, her use of the *Aeneid* throws the novel out of focus and invites speculation on Vergilian parallels which may or may not be applicable. In her next novel, *The Charioteer*, she will have more success in using a work of literature as a symbolic point of departure.

North Face marks the end of the first stage of Mary Renault's literary career. In the first five novels she was an overreacher torn between the popular and the artistic, often lavishing her stylistic gifts on themes that were frankly *déjà vu*. She had not yet refined her conception of what fiction should be, and the critics who objected to her use of point of view would add that at times she seemed to lose control of her material. In his review of *North Face*, Harrison Smith compared the Renault novel with the mystery story:

> The villains are the neuroses hiding in the depths of the minds of hero and heroine, to be tracked down and put away safely in a cell like so many criminals. In real life they might eventually escape, larger and

more menacing than ever. A part of Miss Renault's art is to convince the reader that there is only happiness in store for her tortured lovers.[19]

The comparison was apt, since each of the novels had some melodramatic twist at the end—Mic's freakish accident in *Promise of Love,* Pedlow's incriminating letter in *Kind Are Her Answers,* the passage from the *Lysis* which explained Leo's aversion to the physical in *The Middle Mist,* Mrs. Fleming's disclosure about her first husband in *Return to Night,* Ellen's admission of her frigidity and her neurotic devotion to Jock in *North Face.* Yet for the most part the author did insist on a happy ending, as if the alternative were too painful to consider.

It was inevitable that Mary Renault would soon turn to the world of ancient Greece; the classical cyclorama that loomed over her contemporary novels indicated a personal tension between past and present. That Mary Renault was both in and out of her element can be seen in Neil's parable of postwar *tristesse* that also reflects the author's own disenchantment:

> People get together in this century like insects under a stone, to sanction all their more disgusting emotions and waste most of their good ones. If you can't live without a bit of group-ego, go to a party and get tight. That's honest anyway, you keep your own hangover and the damage to your mind is mainly physical. The Greeks knew that; that's why they honoured Dionysus as a god. The good shepherd who led the beast in mankind into the woods till it was tired, and kept the altars of the immortals pure. [P. 140]

2

Eros and Clio: *The Charioteer* and *The Last of the Wine*

It was only a matter of time before Mary Renault would write a mythic novel in which a classical situation would be used as the medium for examining a contemporary one. In a sense, she attempted such a novel in *The Middle Mist* where Plato's *Lysis* became the standard against which Leo's frustrated Hellenism was to be measured. Unfortunately, the *Lysis* was introduced at the end of the book and consequently became a learned excrescence instead of a permeating symbol. In *The Charioteer* (1953) Mary Renault will use another dialogue, the *Phaedrus*; but now she will orchestrate her Platonism so that it progresses rhythmically from a few muted motifs to a deceptively tranquil coda.

The Charioteer has an interesting history. Americans would have first read it in 1959 when the author was already an established writer of historical fiction; yet it was actually published in England in 1953. Mary Renault brought it to her American publisher, William Morrow & Company, who rejected it because of its frank depiction of homosexuality. (The author equates its rejection with the rise of McCarthyism!) She then submitted her next two novels, *The Last of the Wine* and *The King Must Die*, to Pantheon Books, a division of Random House, which has remained her publisher ever since. On the strength of her reputation, Pantheon published *The Charioteer*, believing that America was finally ready for a novel about British homosexuals in World War II. The situation is even more ironic when one considers that the June 1948 *Partisan Review* carried Leslie Fiedler's now classic essay, "Come Back to the Raft Ag'in, Huck Honey!" which made the astute observation that overt homosexuality would explode the American myth of chaste male love, for it would render suspect four of man's most sacred institutions: the firm handshake, the locker room, the fishing trip, and the poker game.

Some New Critics argue that an author's literary career must never be superimposed on his work; his writings should be evaluated on their own merit without the support of history or biography. If this norm were applied to *The Charioteer*, the novel would have to fall under the category of apprentice work; it simply does not reach the level of excellence achieved by her historical fiction. Furthermore, unless the reader knew the details of its publication, he might consider *The Charioteer* as an interruption of the author's novels about antiquity, for in America it appeared between *The King Must Die* (1958) and *The Bull from the Sea* (1962). Yet *The Last of the Wine* (1956), which began the Hellenic phase of her career, is the companion piece to *The Charioteer*. Before Mary Renault described homosexual friendship as an ennobling relationship in a society where love between men was not suspect, she first depicted a similar friendship in a world which made no distinction between male lovers and male whores.

The Charioteer anticipates *The Last of the Wine* and *The King Must Die* in its *Bildungsroman* technique and in its main character's quest for a father-surrogate. Like *Promise of Love*, it is also concerned with the question of *arete* in its double sense of excellence and self-knowledge. In tracing the development of Laurie Odell who gradually learns to accept his homosexuality, Mary Renault is again working from the casebook approach—the only son whose father abandoned him in the crucial fifth year; the "desert of the public school" where his first special friendship bloomed; the unsuccessful attempt at sex with a woman; the unsullied love for another male that was doomed by its uncompromising innocence; the "gay" party where Laurie discovered his values were not those of a simpleminded transvestite; and his final realization that love partakes of the nature of compassion.

Since Mary Renault has chosen to dramatize the case history of an invert, she must examine her character's early childhood and adolescence. Her approach will antagonize only those who would measure such a novel against Gide's *The Immoralist* with which *The Charioteer* cannot compete in subtlety. While comparisons can be made between Michel's lost pastoralism and Laurie's doomed Platonism, *The Charioteer* must be judged by the standards of popular fiction; it is wise, compassionate, and artistically satisfying without being an art novel.

However, the first chapter comes dangerously close to Freudian parody. When Laurie innocently remarks that someday he will marry his mother, one is prepared for the oedipal consequences. In fairness to the author, even Sophoclean irony is not quite so subtle in the post-Freudian age as it was in Periclean Athens. Chapter two is a decided improvement, for Mary Renault has abandoned psychology for symbolism so imperceptibly that one does not even realize that eleven years have elapsed. Laurie, now sixteen, is in a public school where the students guard their close friends as if they were the crown jewels; it is an atmosphere where epicene giddiness and antimasculine coquetry (" 'Would he look at me, do you think?' ") [1] thrive because of a lack of female companionship.

Laurie discovers that Ralph Lanyon, the prefect of his dormitory, is being expelled. The reason for his expulsion at first seems somewhat nebulous, but the discerning reader will know it was because of homosexuality. However, the chapter is written so economically and with ellipses which perfectly convey an adolescent's unfinished thoughts, that one ultimately views the dismissal through Laurie's bewildered eyes.

As a parting gift, Ralph gives Laurie a copy of the *Phaedrus*, which will not only become an expanding symbol but also the Hellenic referent against which the contemporary action will be measured. He warns Laurie that it is a work whose ideals could never be realized in a flawed universe. The section of the *Phaedrus* that has the greatest meaning for Laurie (and the author) is Socrates' description of the tripartite soul. The soul is like a charioteer who drives two horses, one of which is white, the other black. The white horse is high of stature, with agile limbs and a straight profile; he loves honor and temperance and needs no prodding from the charioteer. The black horse is crooked, thick-necked, and lumbering; a companion of insolence and pride, he is indifferent to the whip and the goad. The charioteer symbolizes reason; the white steed, emotion (*thumos*); and the black one, appetite.

The *Phaedrus* becomes the novel's unifying symbol; even when Laurie lies wounded at Dunkirk, he still has Lanyon's copy in his possession. Laurie is now twenty-three; Dunkirk has left him a cripple with one leg shorter than the other. His physical deformity reflects his divided self; torn between reason and desire, he finds himself in the hospital world of *Promise of Love* where everyone acts in accordance with his gender and profession, and where any deviation from either is branded heretical. Like Vivian and Mic who belonged to their genders "rather incidentally," Laurie will soon discover he must be "loyal to humanity if not to his sex" (p. 128).

It is in the hospital where Laurie reaches the first plateau of self-knowledge; in true Platonic fashion, his excellence, or *arete*, will revolve around another male— the conscientious objector, Andrew Raynes. Significantly, the Greek word for manliness or courage is *andreia*. Laurie's name also evokes the Hellenic past; the laurel, sacred to Apollo, crowned the brows of poets and conquerors. When he wants to tell Nurse Adrian that he will always be "different," he is accepting his nature. He also accepts his lameness, for he realizes that it was through his hospitalization that he met Andrew.

Laurie and Andrew will be lover and beloved, but with a difference. In 1940, "the love that dares not speak its name" forced men into an underground. In Plato, Socrates and Phaedrus could speak of love on the banks of the Ilyssus under a shady plane tree and pursue knowledge in a pastoral setting without the stares of onlookers. But Laurie and Andrew must retreat to Mrs. Chivers's garden with its classical yews and beech trees; an inveterate flag-waver, she banishes them when she learns Andrew is a Quaker. To suggest that guiltlessness can only exist in the mythical past, Mary Renault frames their departure from the garden with two literary excerpts: one from *Paradise Lost* where Adam and Eve leave Eden, and the other from the *Phaedrus* where Socrates compares the soul to a pair of winged horses and a charioteer.

The chapter most readers remember is the sixth with its famous "gay" birthday party, a plot device which Mart Crowley used with equal effectiveness in *The Boys in the Band*. It takes place in a converted nursery, a fitting symbol for some of the infantile actions, including a Senecan suicide attempt, that will transpire there. At the party the wheels of coincidence begin to grind audibly; Laurie is reunited with Ralph Lanyon, who, it seems, brought him back from Dunkirk. It is in this chapter that Mary Renault makes her valuable distinction between men who, despite their psychological handicaps, strive to be males and achieve a certain measure of *andreia*; and men who strive to be women and only succeed in acquiring the worst qualities of the female. Ralph and Laurie are noticeably uncomfortable in the presence of dancing couples and bitchy queens. The entire sequence is a kind of anti-*Symposium* where soggy erudition (an outrageous synopsis of the *Odyssey*) and witless repartee (" 'What's he got that I haven't?' " [p. 122]) prevail over rational discourse.

With the reunion of Ralph and Laurie, a second courtship will begin; Laurie will be forced to choose between Andrew whose innocence would offset his worldliness, and Ralph whose maimed hand would complement his disabled leg.

It would seem that Andrew is Laurie's ideal complement. Their love transcends the physical, and Laurie is satisfied with the mere "contemplation of Andrew's being" (p. 88). Yet Andrew suffers from an ignorance of his own nature. In their first meeting, Laurie tried to discover if Andrew had similar tendencies by making a blatant reference to Tchaikovsky's homosexuality. When he asked Andrew if he thought the composer was "queer," the innocent pacifist showed his total ignorance of the vernacular: " 'Was he? I hadn't heard. He was never actually shut up, surely?' " (p. 50).

With Ralph the situation is different. He knows exactly the kind of world in which he is destined to live:

Ours isn't a horizontal society, it's a vertical one. Plato, Michelangelo, Sappho, Marlowe; Shakespeare, Leonardo, and Socrates if you count the bisexuals— we can all quote the upper crust. But at the bottom —Spud, believe me, there isn't any bottom. Never forget it. You've no conception, you haven't a clue, how far down it goes. [P. 174]

The novel can only end with the union of Ralph and Laurie who complement each other in self-knowledge, which is far more important than experience balanced by innocence. Two men who have fought in battle and have scars to prove it are the real Platonic lovers. Now Ralph and Laurie will be two soldiers who will grow old together.

In a worthless manual called *The Homosexual Handbook* written by someone with the improbable name of Angelo d'Arcangelo, there is a bibliography for inverts seeking consolation in literature; in it, *The Charioteer* is lauded for its "happy ending." Perhaps only a homosexual dreaming of a permanent liaison with his lover would regard the novel as ending happily. Actually, it ends on a twin note of inevitability and resignation. It is a matter of simple arithmetic that when the base of a triangle is removed, the two sides alone remain. Once Andrew withdraws from the *ménage à trois*, Laurie and Ralph are left to pursue a relationship realistically based on one person's need for another; but with Ralph, Laurie will never know the innocent longing he shared with Andrew amid the English beechwoods.

The worn copy of the *Phaedrus* has passed from Laurie to Andrew; with the inevitable union of Laurie and Ralph, Andrew is now, as Socrates would put it, heir to the text as well as the argument. Neither Ralph nor Laurie require its encouragement any longer. The novel has come around full circle, and the author ends

with an epilogue in which the *Phaedrus* theme is re-
stated in poetically controlled language:

> Quietly, as night shuts down the uncertain prospect
> of the road ahead, the wheels sink to stillness in the
> dust of the halting place, and the reins drop from
> the driver's loosened hands. Staying each his hunger
> on what pasture the place affords them, neither the
> white horse nor the black reproaches his fellow for
> drawing their master out of the way. They are far,
> both of them, from home, and lonely, and lengthened
> by their strife the way has been hard. Now their
> heads droop side by side till their long manes mingle;
> and when the voice of the charioteer falls silent they
> are reconciled for a night in sleep. [P. 346]

The prospect is uncertain. In case the reader thinks
Mary Renault is whisking the two lovers off into the
cinematic dusk, he should recall Laurie's final insight
into the nature of his feeling for Ralph: "a deep compassion has the nature of love, which keeps no balance
sheet; we are no longer our own" (p. 346). The Sophoclean inevitability of their union has come to pass, not
out of love, but out of compassion which has "the
nature of love." Like *The Middle Mist* and *Return to
Night*, *The Charioteer* ends tentatively. There can be
no cheerful predictions, for even Plato recognized the
recalcitrant nature of the black steed in all of us.

The Last of the Wine (1956) would have been unthinkable without the six novels that preceded it, especially *The Charioteer*. Manhood and its deterrents
have been the author's preoccupation since *Promise of
Love*. In her previous work, the quest for manhood
was inhibited by an unsympathetic milieu; thus the
novels themselves became inhibited by the omnipresent
classical frame of reference which produced a double,
and sometimes a blurred, vision. A real-ideal polarity

became the axis around which the plot revolved; one saw the characters as they existed in the contemporary world and then wondered how they might have appeared had they lived in antiquity. Moreover, the tension in the characterization often transferred itself to the structure of the novel. When the lovers of *The Charioteer* retreated to the solace of a garden or a car, the reader experienced a similar feeling of confinement; the Hellenic proscenium restricted Laurie, Andrew, and Ralph to a split-level setting where they enacted their drama against a Platonic backdrop.

The next five novels (*The Last of the Wine, The King Must Die, The Bull from the Sea, The Mask of Apollo,* and *Fire from Heaven*) will evidence a greater freedom and an expanded vision that were previously absent. Glory, honor, and excellence are really classical ideals; but in her early work they were pursued by individuals who were historically displaced. In *The Charioteer,* Mary Renault made one last attempt to reconcile a sullied present with an illustrious past; her failure does not point to an artistic defeat, but rather to the mythic novelist's inability to find a suitable world for her Hellenic aspirers. England of 1940 was the wrong milieu; and while the author knew her world well, she was decidedly unsympathetic to its moral restrictions. After a mythic (or better, antimythic) novel like *The Charioteer,* Mary Renault had no other alternative if she was to grow as a writer; she must write about real Greeks in a suitably antique setting. The problems which the characters will encounter in the classical novels will not differ appreciably from those in her early fiction; figures of history and myth had their share of doubts and anxieties. Theseus was distressed by his height, Alexias never knew a father's love, and Athenian homosexuals courted boys as indiscriminately as their British counterparts did. Yet Theseus could compensate for his shortness by becoming the national hero of Athens; and Alexias could openly consummate his love for Lysis without resorting to Laurie Odell's tactic of rumpling the linen of an unused bed to conceal the fact that he and Ralph Lanyon had not slept in separate rooms. Unlike Laurie and Ralph, Alexias and Lysis can achieve excellence and glory because their society had made such goals possible.

It is not merely sufficient for an author to find a world compatible with his artistic temperament and sympathies; he must also work out a style that will define the period he is recreating. In her classical novels, Mary Renault has accomplished both ideals. The style of *The Last of the Wine* approximates Greek usage without schoolboy literalness or stilted elegance. In a Hellenic setting, participles and absolute constructions can be justified and even required; in a contemporary novel they would be branded as awkward or archaic. Her research has resulted in an uncannily accurate reproduction of the Attic style:

> Alexias having died before the time of his marriage, my father now decided to name after him the child that was being born, if it should be a boy. My elder brother Philokles, who was two years old, had been a particularly fine strong child at his birth: but I, when held up by the midwife, was seen to be small, wizened and ugly; my mother having brought me forth nearly a month too soon, either through a weakness of her body or the foreknowledge of a god.[2]

Historical fiction has its own critical canon which demands a creative use of sources, the interweaving of character and event, and particularly a point of view that would be valid for the era in question. Mary Renault is writing a novel that roughly covers the period of the Peloponnesian War (431–404 B.C.). She is ordering her material like an ancient historian turned novelist. Her use of the first person is deceptive; although it would seem that "I narration" imparts a sense of immediacy to historical fiction, the real reason for its presence in *The Last of the Wine* is that the novel is a memoir, as one discovers at the end. Mary Renault's narrative method owes nothing to first person works like *Henry Esmond* or *Tristram Shandy*. It does, however, owe much to Herodotus and Plutarch, neither of whom ever achieved the depersonalization of the self that scientific historiography required; they wrote artistic history interlaced with elements of fiction (tales, anecdotes, dialogues, *exempla*, character sketches, invented speeches). Herodotus in particular anticipates nineteenth-century European fiction with his concept of history as tragedy where the fate of people like Xerxes mirrors the Aeschylean pattern of Hybris, Ate, and Nemesis. Mary Renault has also isolated the seeds of tragedy in the disintegration of the Periclean ideal through imperialism and the perversion of excellence.

While Alexias, the son of a wealthy landowner Myron, is the narrator, he is not omniscient, even though he is composing an autobiography. Like Augustine in the *Confessions*, Alexias is gradually unfolding the events of his life as he shapes them into art; his omniscience is submerged in the narrative where it remains as a historical reflector. Also, the omniscient narrator was unknown in ancient fiction, and if Mary Renault were to employ one, her novel would have a sophistication that would be anachronistic.

Alexias is really a narrator-agent;[3] through his vision, the author presents a historical pageant where figures like Plato, Critias, Xenophon, and Socrates assume lifelike dimensions as they are remembered by one who knew them. Alexias also serves another purpose. A good deal of our information about the Socratic circle is in the form of anecdotes from Plutarch, Diogenes Laertius, Macrobius, and Athenaeus. The anecdotal did play an important role in Graeco-Roman historiography; while some of the ancient *vitae* strike one today as ludicrous and little more than *chronique scandaleuse*, they do constitute a body of fact embellished by myth which the historical novelist cannot ignore. In *The Last of the Wine*, Mary Renault cleverly weaves this anecdotal material into her narrative. While the anecdotes previously existed as mere *obiter dicta*, they now become historically viable (if not verifiable) in a dramatic context where the narrator-agent's experiences give them a credibility which they did not originally possess.

In his quest for knowledge, Socrates, who resembled the satyr Silenus, supposedly attended class with young boys. The tale may well be apocryphal, but Mary Renault seizes upon it as a device to introduce the young Alexias to the master philosopher. The other children laugh at their aged fellow student, but Alexias is fascinated by him. When Alexias expresses a wish to steal eggs from a bird's nest, Socrates warns him against it on the basis of an admonition from his inner voice or *daimonion*. Through one seemingly trivial anecdote, Mary Renault has combined history and characterization. The story of Socrates in the classroom has enabled her to dramatize Alexias' need for a father substitute, Socrates' mesmerizing effect on the young, his Silenus mask which concealed the soul of a divinity, and his mysterious *daimonion* which frequently checked him even in minor matters.

While the anecdotal can deepen characterization, it can also explain certain qualities of historical figures. In her student days Mary Renault was an avid reader of Plato, whose *Dialogues* contained some finely etched portraits of members of the Socratic circle. As Alexias matures, he becomes a disciple of Socrates and thus comes in contact with many of the figures in the eponymous dialogues including Plato's uncle Charmides, his mother's cousin Critias, and the young Phaedo.

The novelist's depiction of Phaedo may offend some of the more prudish classicists because it is drawn from anecdotal material that is hardly edifying. There was a tradition that Phaedo was an Elean captive who worked in an Athenian brothel.[4] Through Socrates' intervention, he was ransomed by either Cebes or Crito. Like *The Charioteer, The Last of the Wine* reflects the distinction between homosexual friendship and homosexual lust. Mary Renault will use the tale of Phaedo as a male prostitute, but hardly for sensational purposes. First she will change his birthplace from Elis to Melos to connect his fate with the outrage that was inflicted on that Dorian island in 415 B.C. Melos wished to remain neutral during the Peloponnesian War, and in retaliation the Athenians killed all males of military age, sold the women and children into slavery, and then colonized the island. As one of the captives, Phaedo was purchased by a brothel-keeper.

Admirers of Plato's *Phaedo* with its exalted view of the soul might shudder at the thought that the innocent youth whose hair Socrates loved to stroke was really a male whore. In the novel, Phaedo is skeptical about the soul's immortality: " 'The soul is a surfeit-dream . . . of a man with food and drink in him and his lust fed' " (p. 100). Always the psychologist, Mary Renault is suggesting that Phaedo's initial skepticism was the result of a profession where only the flesh mattered. That he became the spokesman for Socrates' views on immortality should be construed as a tribute to his conversion.

The intersection of history and fiction is clearly seen in her interpretation of the circumstances surrounding the death of Critias (Kritias), the most ruthless of the Thirty Tyrants. Historically, he was slain at the Battle of Monychia Hill when Thrasybulus (Thrasybulos) led his attack against the oligarchs in 403 B.C. In *The Last of the Wine*, Critias appears as one of Phaedo's clients; to the historian Xenophon, Critias was little more than an ill-mannered pederast interested only in seducing the young Euthydemus (Euthydemos). One day to embarrass him, Socrates commented in the presence of others: "Critias seems to have the desires of a pig; he can no more keep himself from Euthydemus than a pig can keep himself from rubbing against stones." [5] The novelist repeats the incident almost verbatim: " 'Have you got swine-fever or what, Kritias, that you come scraping yourself on Euthydemos like a pig on a stone?' " (p. 124).

Later in the novel, Critias murders Myron, and Alexias avenges his father's death. His revenge is doubly sweet, for the oligarch once made indecent advances to Alexias in his father's house. Alexias and his father are both fictitious characters, but in attributing Critias' death to Alexias, Mary Renault is exercising the prerogative of the historical novelist who can resort to probability in the absence of specific information.

Mary Renault makes her best use of ancient biography in her portrait of Plato, whom she introduces in a completely nonchalant way. Lysis is impressed by the prowess of a young wrestler by the name of Aristocles, but the athlete strikes Alexias as being "too square for beauty" (p. 121). When the wrestler reappears in the plot, we learn that his nickname is Plato. Those versed in ancient philosophy will smile knowingly at the name of Aristocles, for Plato was indeed a nickname meaning "broad-shouldered."

Her Plato is also a would-be poet whom Socrates converted to philosophy. There are, however, some poems ascribed to Plato in the *Greek Anthology*, one of which Mary Renault incorporates into the plot of her novel. According to Diogenes Laertius, Plato was attracted to a youth named Aster ("Star"), who joined him in the study of astronomy. Diogenes quotes the two epigrams Plato wrote for Aster, the more famous of which contains a delicate paranomasia on the boy's name:

> Before you shone as the Morning Star among the living;
> Now you shine as the Evening Star among the dead.

The novelist describes Plato's attraction to Aster, whom he first saw leading a procession of boys. Since it was Alexias who noticed Plato's interest in the youth, it might seem that the narrator-agent is merely the medium for the fictionalization of another anecdote. Yet Mary Renault never brings in a tale for its own sake. Sometime later, Alexias learns from Euthydemus that Aster is dead. When Alexias visits the tomb, he notes the following epitaph:

> Lightbringing dawn star, kindled for the living;
> Bright torch of Hesperos, sinking to the dead.
>
> [P. 306]

The novelist has placed the Aster poem in a human context. The distich is clearly a sepulchral epigram; Mary Renault has rescued it from the *Greek Anthology* where it lay hidden in a mass of similar poems and used it as a means of characterization. The Plato who could lament the passing of a youth is also the Plato who could grieve with equal intensity for the death of Dion of Syracuse. She therefore assumes that the poems ascribed to Plato in the *Greek Anthology* are genuine. Since she is sensitive to Greek nuance, her translation of the Aster poem is a distillation of the epigram's deceptively simple art. The Greek verb *phthinein* can mean either "to waste away" or "to wane"; *en phthimenois* literally means "among those having died or waned." "Sinking to the dead" conveys the ambivalence perfectly and complements the rise-set, life-death imagery.

Like her other historical portraits, Mary Renault's Xenophon is also the result of an imaginative interpretation of historical data. The handbooks present a somewhat bland image of the Athenian who entered the service of Cyrus the Younger and led the Ten Thousand from Cunaxa through Armenia to the Black Sea, and finally to Byzantium. If the name of Xenophon is known at all, it usually evokes memories of his *Anabasis* with its genitive absolutes and duals. Yet Mary Renault has based her characterization of Socrates largely on Xenophon's *Memorabilia*; in fact, she admits that the inspiration for *The Last of the Wine* came from her own attempt to reconcile the Platonic Socrates with the Xenophontic one:

> It happened that just after I had finished [*The Charioteer*] I was reading Xenophon's MEMORA-BILIA OF SOCRATES. I already knew Plato's Dialogues which I used to read in free periods at school, and I was fascinated by the different impression this striking personality made on these two different men, like mirrors reflecting different angles. I began to wonder what the whole group he gathered round him could have been like, with its extraordinary mixture of characters, that brilliant and magnetic scamp Alcibiades, Xenophon, the young Plato later on, the wicked Critias, Phaedo with his tragic history, and so on.[6]

Xenophon endears and exasperates. "I must now speak of pederasty, for it affects education," he declared when he turned to this topic in his analysis of Spartan institutions. To the casual reader, Xenophon was a sober-faced moralist who was enamored of Spartan discipline yet repelled by Spartan pederasty; but to a novelist who uses primary sources to illuminate character, moral values are not inborn. Mary Renault's Xenophon was an ultraconservative even in his youth who staunchly defended the Spartans as God-fearing Greeks against Alexias' indictment of their militarism. Thus his banishment from Athens in 399 B.C. for pro-Spartan sympathies follows logically from his characterization.

In the novel Xenophon speaks in images that are either Spartan or equine. One can readily understand how a manual on horsemanship and *The Constitution of Sparta* could be numbered among his writings. He was also blatantly heterosexual, in contrast to almost everyone else in the novel. Tradition has it that Plato and Xenophon were indifferent to each other; in Xenophon's *Symposium* there is not the paean to boy-love that one finds in Plato's work of the same name. When Alexias recalls that "one never saw Xenophon paying court to a youth, nor Plato to a woman" (p. 241), his distinction indicates that the author has not only mastered her scholarship but that she has also caught an essential difference between the two biographers of Socrates. Understandably, only Xenophon could make the brilliant comparison between the male body which is naturally suited to military campaigns and the female's which is designed for indoor tasks.[7]

A novel set in the period of the Peloponnesian War should make some reference to Pericles' Funeral Oration which he delivered in 430 B.C. over those who had fallen in the first year of the conflict. The speech is found in Thucydides, but no historical novelist could improve upon its faultless rhetoric. The oration, however, was never delivered in its present form; all the speeches in Thucydides were invented and idealized, although they undoubtedly followed the general lines of what was actually said. Since Mary Renault is conveying the point of view of an eyewitness who heard the original oration, she records with acute irony the circumstances under which it was delivered and the impression it left on the seven-year-old Lysis:

> I stared at the high wooden rostrum they had built for Perikles, waiting for him to climb it, as children wait for a show. When he appeared, I admired his dignity and his fine helmet; and the first sound of his voice struck a kind of thrill upon my ear. But soon I grew tired of standing. . . . I was glad when it was over, and if you had asked me a year later to quote the speech of Perikles, I doubt if I could have fished you up a dozen words. [P. 224]

While the novelist explodes some venerable myths and creates characters from biographical anecdotes, her use of factual material is unassailable. The first really historical incident in the novel is the mutilation of the Hermae which occurred in May, 415 B.C. On the eve of the Sicilian Expedition, the Hermae, square pillars with busts of the god Hermes which stood at the entrances of temples and private homes in Athens, were mutilated. Because of his profanation of the Eleusinian Mysteries and other acts of debauchery, Alcibiades was thought to be the instigator of the sacrilege. But Alexias and Lysis are too intelligent to believe that he was implicated in the affair. When Lysis tells Alexias that Alcibiades is innocent, he is echoing modern scholarship which lays the blame on drunken youths bent on desecration.

To Alexias, the conflict between Athens and Sparta was the Great War, and many historians have compared it with World War I. Following Thucydides, Mary Renault describes the young Athenians gaily rushing off to join the Sicilian Expedition as if it were a war of liberation. A comparison between the novelist and her Greek source will show how historical fact can be transformed into artistic fiction without the loss of truth:

> Practically all of Athens, citizens and foreigners alike, went down to the Piraeus. The natives were there to see off their friends, relatives or sons (whatever the case may be), hoping for conquest and at the same time lamenting those who might never be seen again; for it was a long voyage on which they were being sent. While they were taking leave of each other, the danger of the situation struck closer to home than it did when they were voting for the expedition; but their courage revived when they saw the strength and magnitude of the fleet. The foreigners and the rest of the crowd, on the other hand, came purely for the spectacle, thinking it would be notable and beyond belief. [Thucydides, *History of the Peloponnesian War*, 6. 30. 2]

> The cheering began in the City . . . and crept towards us between the Long Walls. Then it roared through Piraeus; one could hear the music coming, and shield clashing on corselet to the beat. Now you could see between the Walls the helmet-crests moving, a river of them, a long snake bright with his new scales in springtime, bronze and gold, purple and red. Sparks of light seemed to dance above it, the early sun catching the points of many thousand spears; the dust-cloud shone like powdered gold. On the roofs . . . the foreigners were . . . marvelling at the beauty and might of the army. . . . Kinsmen and friends ran up for last farewells. [*The Last of the Wine*, p. 37]

Thucydides emphasized the diversified audience at the Piraeus, the air of national pride mingled with despondency, and the distinction between the Athenians who were sending their own to be killed and the foreigners who had assembled to witness a grand spectacle. Mary Renault translates these facts into a striking vignette. The procession which began with cheering in the distance unfolded like a serpent's coils. She enlarges the Thucydidean snyopsis into a *son et lumière* which in itself is an indictment of the spurious nationalism the expedition engendered.

Like Thucydides, she depicts the aftermath of the Sicilian disaster with seven thousand Athenians left to die of starvation and disease in the Syracusan rock quarries:

> At first the Syracusans treated the prisoners cruelly in the stone quarries. Packed together in large numbers in a deep and narrow pit, they were exposed to the sun and suffocating heat, for there was no roof. Then in sharp contrast there were the cool autumn nights; the sudden drop in temperature produced disease. Lack of space required that everything be done in the same place. Moreover, the dead were piled one on another, some having died of their own wounds, others from the change of temperature or similar causes. As a result the odor was intolerable. At the same time they were suffering from hunger and thirst; for eight months the Syracusans allotted them only half a pint of water and a pint of corn. . . . For seventy days they all lived like this; then all the rest, except for the Athenians and Greeks from Italy and Sicily who joined the expedition, were sold. [Thucydides, 7. 87]

> The quarries at Syracuse are deep. They lived there without shelter from the scorching sun or the frosts of the autumn nights. . . . The dust filled their hair,

and the wounds of the dying, and the mouths of the dead. . . . There was nowhere in the rock to dig them graves . . . but because a fallen man takes up more room than one on his feet, they piled them into stacks. . . . After a time not much work was demanded of them, for no overseer could . . . endure the stench. For food they were given a pint of meal a day, and for drink half a pint of water. . . . After about two months the Syracusans took away the allied troops . . . and sold them off. They kept the Athenians in the quarry. [*The Last of the Wine*, pp. 144–45]

Mary Renault's uniqueness does not consist solely in her talent for interpreting sources creatively; she also assumes the moral attitudes of the post-Periclean world she has reconstructed. Nowhere is her ability to immerse herself in the Greek ethos more evident than in her treatment of homosexuality. She makes no attempt to justify the practice but presents it as a given. However, Socrates distinguished between homosexual lovers pursuing the ideal of *philia* and those who merely lusted after youths. *The Last of the Wine* will reflect this distinction. Alexias' father, who was once the beloved of Alcibiades, explains the phenomenon of the courtship to his son as if it were a fact of life; he tells his son that he must first deserve his suitors but under no circumstances should he succumb to gifts and flattery. While Myron can accept a relationship between an older man and a youth, he cannot tolerate males who sell their favors. His double standard was essentially Socratic; Socrates felt it was prostitution to offer one's beauty indiscriminately, but a mark of virtue to become the lover of a man of honor.[8]

Socrates, in fact, represents the mean between homosexual friendship and loveless sodomy. In Plato's *Sym-*

posium, Alcibiades relates the story of his attempted seduction of Socrates. The story is pointless unless one realizes that Socrates was tempted. While the philosopher delighted in stroking the heads of Charmides and Phaedo and in frequenting the palaestra to see the handsome youths, he subordinated his physical desires to his quest for the beautiful and the good. A Freudian would probably ascribe his enjoyment of young men's company to sexual curiosity, yet Socrates warned against courting lovers for their looks alone: " 'Do you not know that the creature called "young and fair" is more lethal than the scorpion and that he can sting you even at a distance and drive you mad?' " [9] Mary Renault's Socrates also chastizes suitors for "wasting their pains upon uncertainty" (p. 84). The Socratic morality was by no means schizophrenic; there is a difference, and not a superficial one, between a sexually sublimated desire for the company of youths and the indiscriminate courting of them with gifts and poems.

History, whether scientific or anecdotal, is only an ancilla to literature. Above all, *The Last of the Wine* is a novel, and brilliantly conceived one. Like *The Charioteer*, it is a *Bildungsroman* where a young man grows to maturity always knowing that on the day he was born his father wanted to kill him. Alexias' *odi et amo* attitude toward Myron recurs in *The King Must Die* where Theseus harbored similarly ambivalent feelings toward his father, Aegeus. In some respects, the author is still psychoanalyzing the behavior of a young male raised by an unfeeling parent who was more preoccupied with his political club than with the upbringing of his son. For maternal affection, Alexias gravitated to his stepmother who was his own age. Named after his uncle who drank hemlock so he could join his lover in death, Alexias will achieve a similar relationship with Lysis. Like Harmodius and Aristogeiton, the two will attain the Socratic goal of soldiers in a regiment of lovers.

While Alexias has certain traits in common with Mic Freeborn and Julian Fleming, he is basically an Athenian male. He cherishes his stepmother, but he is too much of a Greek to emulate the female who is "ignorant of philosophy and logic, and fearing dream-diviners more than immortal Zeus" (p. 1). Before he marries Thalia, Lysis describes his ideal woman for Alexias; afterward, he encourages his friend to marry as well. When Lysis dies, Alexias marries his widow. In case there is a temptation to regard the marriage as an attempt to perpetuate Lysis' memory, one should realize that a young widow at this time would either become a prostitute or be sold into white slavery. Under such circumstances, the next-of-kin customarily married the widow.

The Last of the Wine even goes beyond the *Bildungsroman*; it is essentially a record of the end of the Athenian democracy which is suggested by three symbols: wine, athletics, and the final torchlight race. The title is derived from the Greek practice of spelling out the name of the beloved with the dregs from the last of the wine. Before he died, Alexias' uncle wrote Philon's name with the lees. Lysis and Alexias also found each other's name in the lees. But wine is a symbol of loss as well as love; it can stain as well as exhilarate.[10] The night on which the Hermae were disfigured resembled "a dark wine when clear water is mixed in" (p. 72). Critias spills wine on Alexias in a clumsy attempt to fondle him. To entice Phaedo to enter his establishment, the brothel-keeper comes to him in the evening with wine.

Concomitant with the end of the democracy was the decline of athletics and art. The two were interrelated since the gymnasium was the Greek sculptor's studio. Socrates was fond of comparing the decline of excellence with overspecialization in athletics. When Lysis enters the Isthmian Games, his opponent is a muscle-bound brute. There is no doubt that by the middle of the fifth century the rise of professionalism made athletics fall out of fashion. One has only to compare fifth- and fourth-century art to notice the difference. Lysippus' *Apoxyomenos*, for instance, depicts an athlete scraping himself with a strigil; his small head and slim body indicate that he is either a jumper or a runner, but not a versatile pancratiast.

In his youth Myron was one of Phidias' models, but Alexias was reduced to posing for a degenerate who offered him a nightly cup of wine. Alexias loathes the sculptor's effeminate Apollos. Mary Renault is clearly thinking about (and condemning) the soft graciousness, sensuous curves, languid poses, and dreamy gazes which Praxiteles introduced.

At the end of the novel, Mary Renault restores Athens to its previous splendor, if only for a moment. The final tableau is a torchlight race which she borrowed from the beginning of the *Republic*. The race in which youths on horseback passed torches to each other in relay fashion symbolized the fire of civilization which must be continually fed; ironically, the last of the wine is also the last of the fire. Plato, Phaedo, Socrates, and Alexias assemble at twilight to watch the performance; but a new character appears, Anytus (Anytos), who will be the chief accuser at Socrates' trial.

As Plato delivers his invective against democracy which he regarded as the worst form of government, Anytus rehearses the charges of impiety and sophistry which he will bring against Socrates at his trial. Anytus' son is also present; he is drunk and audibly vulgar. The wine which once fostered the friendship of lovers reappears with its symbolism a bit sullied but not completely defiled; for in sharp contrast to the drunken obscenities, Socrates stands silhouetted against the sky with a wine cup in his hand.

3

To Be a King: The Theseus Novels

The revival of interest in ancient literature in our century was due to three main factors: psychoanalytic interpretation of myth, archaeological finds, and anthropological criticism of the Classics. Despite the inaccuracies of *Totem and Taboo*, Freud's thesis that the Oedipus complex was at the center of religion, art, society, and ethics has resulted in a neo-Hellenic literature which, despite its limitations, was a continuation of the Greek practice of reworking myth to provide fresh insights into timeless tales. For a civilization endures only as long as people believe in the myths on which it was built. By present standards, some of this Freudian literature strikes one as little more than melodrama lacquered by a thin veneer of bogus Hellenism. Today it would be quite easy to snicker at Lavinia Mannon's Electra complex or to dismiss as obvious the Medea-Phaedra-Oedipus parallels in *Desire under the Elms*. Still, there have been many fine works—Cocteau's *The Infernal Machine*, Giraudoux's *Electra*, Jeffers's *The Tower beyond Tragedy*, to cite a few—which would have been unthinkable without Freud's reinterpretation of myth.

While the psychoanalytic approach has given the figures of myth an archetypal and a literary prominence, archaeology established the environments in which they lived. From 1900 to his death in 1941, the world of Sir Arthur Evans centered about the excavations at Knossos in Crete where, largely at his own expense, he reconstructed the fabled Palace of Minos. Gide was certainly familiar with Evans' work; in his *Theseus*, there are some ravishingly accurate descriptions of Late Minoan attire which cannot be attributed solely to his sensuous imagination. When Joyce was writing *A Portrait of the Artist as a Young Man*, he might have read about the early stages of the Knossos excavations from reports in the London *Times*. However, it is more likely that his interest in the Theseus myth stemmed from D'Annunzio's *The Flame*. Still it is significant that he interwove labyrinth and minotaur imagery throughout the *Portrait*.

Gide's Theseus, however, is not a fleshed out character; rather he is the personification of the indomitable spirit of the humanist whose Dostoevskian farewell, *j'ai vécu*, marks the end of a life of high adventure and personal tragedy. Joyce's *Portrait*, with all its Daedalian motifs, is classical only in its epigraph and imagery. It remained for Mary Renault to combine her knowledge of myth, archaeology, anthropology, and Freud to produce a colorful romance in the grand tradition of Flaubert's *Salammbô*.

In a sense it would seem that she has chosen one of the more unspectacular figures of antiquity. Compared to his cousin Hercules (Heracles), his wife Phaedra, and his son Hippolytus, Theseus never had much of a literary vogue. In extant Greek drama he appears in Sophocles' *Oedipus at Colonnus* and in three Euripidean plays: *The Suppliants*, *Hippolytus*, and *The Madness of Heracles*; but in none of these is he the protagonist. Hercules, however, achieved genuine tragic stature in Sophocles' *Women of Trachis* and *The Madness of Heracles*; and Phaedra's infatuation with her stepson has a literary tradition of its own ranging from *Hippolytus* (428 B.C.) to Frank Gilroy's *That Summer, That Fall* (1967). Poets have found his friendship with Pirithous worthy of note, but for the most part Theseus is usually discussed in relation to someone else. Even Shakespeare in *A Midsummer Night's Dream* had difficulty in delineating this faceless hero and was content to draw him as a typical Renaissance nobleman. Eclipsed on the one hand by his relatives and on the other by his exploits, Theseus hardly seems the ideal hero for a mythological novel. Yet he is Mary Renault's most fully realized character.

In one way it is understandable that she would be attracted to him. Her male characters are either products of a society that demands proof of manhood in the most elementary way, or else they are victims of a matriarchal environment that makes normal sexuality impossible without the help of an understanding woman. Theseus differs from the others in one major way: his masculinity was strengthened rather than stultified by a matrilinear society. Again the author is reminding us that in antiquity a male could transcend the Cult of the Mother and fulfill his manhood by traversing a heroic path which the twentieth century would equate with an obstacle course.

Only to a purist is myth sacrosanct. The ancients even modified their legends as age or vision dictated. Euripides' Achilles in *Iphigenia in Aulis* is as different from Homer's as the period of the Sophists is from the Bronze Age. In *Troilus and Cressida*, Shakespeare suggested an actual relationship between Achilles and Patroclus that only existed as an emotional attachment in the *Iliad*. In *The Infernal Machine*, Cocteau's Sphinx is a young girl in search of love, and Jocasta a nymphomaniac who calls Tiresias Zizi. Gladys Schmitt actually dispensed with Clytemnestra's murder by her children in *Electra*, preferring to stress the loneliness that will result when brother and sister go their separate ways.

Mary Renault will also take liberties with the Theseus myth since she is doing more than retelling ancient legend. She is actually charting the development of a hero and his arduous ascent to self-knowledge. Such an approach immediately sets her apart from the pulp mythographers who merely tell a story as fancifully as possible. Yet not all heroes are like Hermes, who within a few hours of his birth had already stolen some of Apollo's cattle. To Mary Renault it is only in the fullness of time that true heroism is seen.

It is this concept of the gradual unraveling of *moira*, or personal destiny, that dominates *The King Must Die* (1958); and it is the same concept, so strikingly Hellenic, that has made the academicians gravitate to Mary Renault for light reading but rarely with the idea of making her fiction the subject of a serious study. Somehow literature where ancient myth is superimposed on a contemporary situation (Murdoch's *A Severed Head*, Robbe-Grillet's *Erasers*) engenders more excitement among scholars than an old-fashioned romance. The reason may very well be that in mythic literature, as distinguished from mythological, there is more room for creative speculation (there always is in a crossword puzzle without a key) and less for laborious source-hunting.

Mary Renault had no other choice but to set her novel in antiquity. A hero's consenting to his *moira* or his close identification with an Olympian would be incomprehensible in a modern setting. Yet it is precisely the setting that has kept her out of the literary journals; a novel about archaic Greece conjures up the ghosts of *Ben Hur* and *The Last Days of Pompeii*—fine bedside reading but not to be taken seriously. However, *The King Must Die*, apart from being her finest work, also deserves to be ranked among the best re-creations of the Hellenic past, for it fulfills the primary requisite of mythopoetic art: the re-creation of a world where the author's vision is supplemented by a historical sense linking the individual talent with the tradition that has preceded it. Furthermore, her achievement in *The King Must Die* cannot be measured by the standards of contemporary historical fiction; no other writer of this genre includes an Author's Note, a mythological sketch, and a bibliography. While other novelists employ the epigraph, few have welded it so closely to the narrative. The epigraph is, in fact, the key to her literary technique which is completely Homeric in language and incident.

The epigraph comes from the *Iliad* (1. 352–53); it is Achilles' outcry against the short life for which he is fated: "Oh, Mother! I was born to die soon; but Olympian Zeus the Thunderer owes me some honor for it." The excerpt requires that the novel be viewed within the framework of the Homeric hero's need for *kudos*, the glory that will make him immortal. But there is a note of insistence in Achilles' words; Zeus *owes* him some honor for his brief life. Although Achilles was the son of the mortal Peleus and the sea nymph Thetis, it is really Zeus who is his patron deity in the *Iliad*. Thus Achilles can make demands of Zeus in much the same way as a son can claim his birthright from his father. Mary Renault will apply Achilles' relationship with Zeus to Theseus' identification with his tutelary deity, Poseidon. Achilles' desire for *kudos* will become the basis of Theseus' quest for kingship. While the *Iliad* supplied the author with an archetypal relationship between a hero and a god, it was only the point of departure for *The King Must Die*. When the *Iliad* opens in the tenth year of the Trojan War, Achilles' character is already formed; Homer says nothing of his youth since it has no bearing on his wrath. *The King Must Die*, on the other hand, begins with Theseus at the age of seven witnessing an event that was to provide him with his first insight into *moira* and *kudos*: the sacrifice of the King Horse.

It is in the opening of the novel that one sees how a historical novelist works from her source. Plutarch's *Life of Theseus* says nothing of such an event; yet horses were slain in honor of Poseidon, and the animal sacrifice is a common occurrence in Homer. To the ancients, it was a good omen if the animal died obediently, or to use one of the author's favorite words, "consenting." Mary Renault's approach to myth is essentially psychological. At the heart of her Theseus portrait is the mythmaker's question: What would be the effect of a ritualistic sacrifice on the mind of a seven-year-old boy? All too often the contemporary reader takes for granted what he reads in Homer and dismisses the ordering of hecatombs as a mere epic convention. Yet a hero does not acquire the instinct for *kudos* by infused knowledge; it grows within him as a result of what he has seen as a child. If Achilles grew up in a society where "faultless hecatombs" were sacrificed, he would soon realize that renown is the only alternative for the brevity of life. No doubt when the animal bowed its head in acquiescence, Achilles also learned something about the nature of *moira*.

The slaying of the sacrificial animal was often an elaborate ceremony. Jane Harrison, one of the "Cambridge anthropologists" who, along with Gilbert Murray, argued for a ritual background for Greek tragedy, described such a ceremony. Drawing upon inscriptional evidence as well as the testimony of Pausanias, she has reconstructed a bull sacrifice in which the animal was led in procession to the place of dedication. Coins showing the bull kneeling or bowing its head suggest some sign was required that the animal was offering itself freely before it could be slain.[1]

Mary Renault works from the findings of historians of religion, but she also realizes that the novelist must transform his source material into art. The sacrifice of the King Horse is anthropologically accurate, but the art with which she describes it is completely her own. She takes her cue from one of Homer's best-loved epithets, "rosy-fingered dawn," and weaves this image throughout her description. The sacrifice begins at dawn, and the palace at Troezen is bathed in roseate light: "Morning was red, and the crimson-painted columns burned in it." [2] Theseus puts on a red belt and glances at the pink tips of his mother's breasts. The warriors in the procession "shone russet in the rosy light"; the gold of their attire mingles sensuously with the red of the dawn, and the combined symbols of royalty and death coalesce in a strikingly effective union.

The King Horse symbolizes the Achillean short but glorious life. As Theseus' first recollection, it has a threefold purpose. First, he learns the need to accept his *moira* which his grandfather explains to him in the language of the potter's craft: " 'The finished shape of our fate, the line drawn round it. It is the task the gods allot us, and the share of glory they allow; the limits we must not pass; and our appointed end. Moira is all these' " (p. 17). Second, the King Horse with whom he feels a certain kinship dies in his prime before he is eclipsed by a younger rival. It is significant that at the end of *The Bull from the Sea*, Theseus will prefer death while his heroic stature is still undiminished. Lastly, the sacrifice paves the way for Theseus' identification with Poseidon, a point which requires further elucidation.

One of the most difficult obstacles to surmount in

understanding archaic Greece is the identification of hero and deity, especially as it exists in Homer. The handbooks state that the gods are mortals possessing immortality and bleeding ichor instead of blood; actually, Homer's deities have more in common with humans than they do with each other. Far from being epic ornaments, the Olympians are, as one scholar described them, "symbolic predicates of action, character, and circumstance." [3]

The interrelationship between god and mortal in Homer is not arbitrary; the gods favor mortals with whom they have something in common. The crafty Pallas Athena befriends "Odysseus of the many wiles"; Zeus' aloofness from his fellow Olympians parallels Achilles' withdrawal from the war. Thus the Theseus-Poseidon relationship is perfectly acceptable in terms of a polytheistic religion or even a monotheistic one with a plurality of saints; the devotee chooses a god or a saint with whom he has something in common or with whom a bond of sympathy exists. After the sacrifice of the King Horse, Theseus is dedicated to Poseidon who becomes his special deity, patron, benefactor, and model.

In addition to being a sea divinity, Poseidon was worshipped under various names. He was called *Hippios*, a god of horses, and was often revered in equine form because of a myth which claimed he pursued Demeter in the shape of a stallion. He is also *Ennosiagios*, the Earth-Shaker. The ancients originally thought that the eroding of the ground by subterranean rivers caused earthquakes, and consequently the god of water was also the god of earthquakes. Furthermore, the Greeks sacrificed bulls to Poseidon because they imagined river deities as bull-like in strength. Thus horses, earthquakes, and bulls will figure prominently in Theseus' life. At the end of the sacrifice he feels Poseidon's presence as the sound of the sea whirs in his ears; it is a sound that will recur in the novel. Then Poseidon gives him the gift of predicting earthquakes in compensation for the taunts he received about his dubious parentage. Finally there is the bull which will take on greater significance when Theseus reaches Crete.

Mary Renault's characterization of Theseus answers many of the problems in the original myth. A boy short of stature would invariably be attracted to a deity who was the personification of manliness and strength. A boy who grew up without a father would also find in Poseidon an ideal substitute, for the god embodied all the qualities which most sons would find worthy of emulation: sexual potency, physical endurance, and a majestic awesomeness. The novelist's psychological approach also forbids her incorporating the fanciful and the supernatural into her narrative. Traditionally, Aegeus (Aigeus) slept with Aethra (Aithra), a Troezen princess, on the same night as Poseidon did. Theseus was the result of that twofold conception. Before his son's birth, Aegeus left Troezen after hiding his sword and sandals under a huge rock; Theseus would recover these tokens when he was strong enough to lift the rock. This is the archetypal situation of The Trial and is frequently found in *Märchen*; but its appearance in contemporary fiction is bound to be ludicrous. Since the author is describing the evolution of a hero, she rewrites the myth and has Theseus fail in his first attempt to lift the rock. When he does succeed, it is through the aid of a lever.

The author's originality is even more apparent in her version of Theseus' birth, which is a decided improvement on the myth of double impregnation. The episode embodies motifs from the *Iliad* and *Oedipus the King*, both of which open in time of plague. A pestilence has fallen upon Troezen because Aethra was still a virgin. She must take as her lover the first man who swims across the water to the Myrtle House. Like Leander, Aegeus swam to his beloved in a storm. When he emerged from the water, a bluish light enveloped him; because he resembled the blue-haired Poseidon, the tradition arose that Aethra had conceived by the sea god.

According to Plutarch, Theseus was en route to Athens when Cercyon (Kerkyon) stopped him in Eleusis and challenged him to a wrestling match. Theseus accepted the challenge, lifted his opponent up by the knees and dashed him to the ground. Mary Renault will use a similar incident in book two of *The King Must Die*, but she will interpret it differently. First of all, wrestling is a form of ritual combat, or *agon*, between the Year King and his rival. Second, the event took place at Eleusis, the home of the Eleusinian Mysteries.[4] The author will again pose the mythopoetic question: What were these Mysteries originally?

Few rituals in antiquity are so perplexing to modern scholars. Originally the Mysteries were secret rites conducted at Eleusis, a city fourteen miles northwest of Athens, in honor of the grain goddess, Demeter. They originated as an agrarian cult to promote fertility of the soil and the growth of crops. Then a parallel must have arisen in the primitive mind between the seed which is planted in the soil and the body of man which is buried in the earth. If crops could grow from seed, then man could achieve a similar form of renewal. The Mysteries then moved from an agricultural rite of purification to a cult of immortality which would enable the initiated to face death by experiencing the prospect of a future life. It also seems clear that on one of the days of purification, a passion play was performed depicting Demeter's quest for her lost daughter, Persephone. Certainly the myth of Demeter with its emphasis on loss and restoration mirrors the vegetation cycle of life-death-life.

In the classical period the Eleusinian Mysteries were among the most sublime forms of religious expression, and in *The Bull from the Sea* Mary Renault vividly described the initiated or *mystai* cleansing themselves in the sea in a ritual baptism. But few rites begin on such an exalted note, and in book two ("Eleusis") the author is suggesting that there must have been a stage before the Mysteries achieved a sacramental character, a stage when purification was required to rid the Eleusinians of their guilt in the death of the Year King who was slain as scapegoat and buried in a cornfield.

This is a bold conjecture, and one that is bound to infuriate anti-Frazerites. Mary Renault is assuming that Theseus' encounter with Cercyon at Eleusis was more than just a chance meeting. Cercyon's name is connected with a pig cult; the pig was used in the Eleusinian Mysteries because its blood was considered powerful enough to absorb the impure spirit in men.[5] If one reads Plutarch's *Life of Theseus* concurrently with Robert Graves's *The Greek Myths*, the wrestling bout will naturally emerge as the ritual battle between the Year King and his rival.

In the novel, Theseus arrived in Eleusis on the day when the king must die. Book two is the logical outgrowth of the Book of Troezen; the animal sacrifice Theseus witnessed as a child will recur under the form of the ritual death of the Eleusinian king. He will wrestle with Cercyon, who will also die "consenting." Moreover, the author will follow the traditional anthropological sequence of *agon*, or combat (Cercyon and Theseus); the *pathos*, or sacrificial death of the Year King (the breaking of Cercyon's neck); and the *threnos*, or lamentation (the wailing of the queen and her handmaidens).

Theseus becomes the new Year King, the consort of Queen Persephone. She is, of course, not the wife of

Pluto (Hades) but merely her namesake. Since Theseus is always forced into situations where he must prove his manhood, his fierce independence will not allow him to be Persephone's thrall. He realizes that Eleusis is a matriarchal and matrilinear society where males occupy an inferior position. He organizes the men into a cohort called "The Companions" and establishes a program for them that combines physical training with military drills.

Again Mary Renault will rework myth. In Crommyon, Theseus allegedly slew a sow called Phaea (Phaia), but the novelist transfers the episode to Eleusis. The sow becomes a symbol of the matriarchal society which Theseus must destroy, and the conquest of Phaea is actually described in terms of rape:

> She hated men. As she thrust and jerked and squealed, I knew it was not her own life she fought for; it was mine. Fixed by my slender shaft to this huge force of earth, I felt as light as grass; I was beaten and bruised upon the rock behind me, as if the very mountain were trying to kill me on her breast like a pricking gnat. . . . Then when I braced to the thrust she pulled instead, so that my arm nearly sprang from its socket. I knew I was nearly done. . . . One more great writhe and wallow she gave, that ground the spear butt upon the rock; but it was her death-throe. [P. 95]

In book three, Theseus arrives at Athens where he expects to take his place as his father's heir, but destiny has other plans. It is at this point that the author adds a touch of Platonism to her characterization and casts Theseus in the role of the would-be guardian of the state who must first return to the Cave before he can rule.

While she does not put Theseus through the rigid education in music and gymnastics that are part of the philosopher-king's formation, she does adopt one of Plato's cardinal principles in the *Republic*. At thirty-five, the true guardian of the state should be ready for kingship; but Plato demands that he return to the world of the unenlightened for fifteen years. He may be killed, Plato warns, for those in darkness have learned to hate the light; yet this descent will give him the practical experience that kingship requires. Theseus also believed he was ready to rule, but *moira* demanded a further sacrifice of him. He had arrived at Eleusis when the Year King was to die; now he is in Athens when the fourteen youths and maidens are to be selected by lot as an offering to King Minos. Again he hears the sea sound and realizes it is Poseidon's will that he be part of the tribute. Theseus adds his name to the list, and the period of servitude which will prepare him to assume the rule of Athens begins.

The Book of Crete is one of Mary Renault's finest achievements in fiction; in it she has the opportunity both to revitalize myth and to illustrate her knowledge of archaeology. First she dispenses with the legendary Minotaur, who was the result of Queen Pasiphae's lust for a bull. Instead Pasiphae has a liaison with a bull dancer to whom she bore a son, Asterion, the pretender to the Cretan throne. Having dispensed with the Cretan monster, she will use her knowledge of the Knossos excavations to explain the traditional sacrifice to the Minotaur. She has apparently studied some of the frescoes in the Palace at Knossos which were restored by the Swiss artist, Gilliéron. One of them depicted a youth somersaulting over the back of a charging bull while a girl matador waited behind the animal's flank to catch him. Other frescoes showed elaborately attired Cretan women sitting in box seats watching some spectacle. Perhaps the scene was a bullring where the young matadors exhibited their skill. Leonard Cottrell has posed the rhetorical question which Mary Renault has answered: "Were these young men and girls the Athenian hostages who, according to tradition, were sent each year as tribute to the Minotaur?" [6]

The fourteen hostages will become the Cranes, a team of bull-leapers and bull-catchers, performing a sport which the Cretan nobility apparently relished. In the novel, the team must capture its own bull by using a cow as decoy. Interestingly enough, a golden cup was found at Vapheio which showed a bull being netted while a cow stood passively by, her tail raised in sexual excitement. In fact, everything about Mary Renault's depiction of the Palace at Knossos is accurate—the russet columns, double axes, storerooms with great earthenware jars, the griffin-frescoed Throne Room, a Central Court with porticoes and galleries that may have been the setting for the bull games, and even the monkeys painted on the wall of Phaedra's bedroom. In one episode that stands as a model of iconography, Ariadne appears before Theseus attired as the Mother Goddess. The model was the famous figurine of the Cretan Snake Goddess, who was dressed in a tight-waisted crinoline skirt; her breasts were bare, and each outstretched hand held a writhing serpent.

But the serpents Ariadne holds have been defanged. She is not a true priestess, for the rite she performs is a fraud. Her half brother Asterion is equally fraudulent, for he plans to rule Crete after Minos' death without divine sanction. Peter Wolfe argued that Ariadne's bogus fertility ritual and Asterion's political machinations symbolized the decadence of Minoan Crete. [7] Theseus is horrified at such religious and political corruption, for his standards are basically Homeric. In Homer's aristocratic society, the power of the king (*basileus*), although limited, still was considered as coming from Zeus.

Minos' leprosy further reflects Crete's moral decay. As his successor, Theseus must first slay Minos who, like the King Horse and Cercyon, consents to die. He must also kill Asterion, and here Mary Renault gives another original interpretation to an archaeological find. Scholars believe that an earthquake destroyed Knossos about 1400 B.C., yet the excavations have revealed that an anointing ceremony which seems to have been interrupted violently was taking place in the Throne Room at about the same time. The earthquake will occur in the novel, and the ceremony will be Asterion's investiture. Employing the sinuous movements of the bull dance, Theseus encircles Asterion and slays him.

The Book of Naxos should dispel any notion that Mary Renault is a romanticist. In most versions, Theseus abandoned Ariadne on Naxos where Dionysus (Dionysos) took her as his bride. Music lovers might recall the end of Richard Strauss's *Ariadne auf Naxos*, in which Bacchus (Dionysus) and his beloved ascend the heavens where Ariadne is transfigured into a constellation. Mary Renault's Dionysus is not the Straussian hero seeking redemption through a woman, nor is he the jolly Bacchus of the Romans. Rather he is the god of Euripides' *Bacchae*, a god who can drive his votaries to such a frenzied pitch that they dismember animals and humans. In his *Theseus*, Gide wittily remarked that Ariadne's rescue by Dionysus might have been a way of saying that she found consolation in drink. Mary Renault may well have taken her cue from Gide, for her Ariadne finds permanent satisfaction in the Dionysian cult.

Again Theseus arrives in a land when the king must die. The Naxian king is the year's scapegoat whom the worshippers of Dionysus dismember. Ariadne joins their rite, and when Theseus sees her afterward, she is asleep —her breath reeking of wine, her teeth bloodstained, and one hand clutching a piece of the king's flesh.

The episode is vital to the novel, for it completely destroys the romanticism of the "Ariadne Abandoned" tradition. Again the novelist has asked the mythmaker's question: What did Dionysus' arrival at Naxos really mean? The answer is simply that he brought his worship with him; and if Ariadne became his bride, she would then be one of his followers. What Mary Renault has described does not differ from the worship Euripides depicted in the *Bacchae* where Agave in her ecstatic frenzy participated in the decapitation of her own son. In a way, the Naxian orgy complements Titian's awesome vision of "Dionysian frivolity" in his *Bacchus and Ariadne* where one ivy-crowned celebrant brandishes a horse's hoof and another is entwined with serpents.

Mary Renault's interpretation of Theseus' return is even more myth-shattering than her view of Ariadne as Maenad. In legend, Theseus was a forgetful hero. As he approached the Attic coast, he "forgot" to change the color of his sails from black to white, and in despair his father threw himself into the sea. Mary Renault's hero is motivated by the overriding goal of kingship. He is well aware of the bargain he made with Aegeus before leaving for Crete. On the one hand, it would seem that the hoisting of a white sail would be an easy task. But Theseus begins to rationalize, subjecting a simple agreement between father and son to a hairsplitting semantic analysis. He literally ducks under a wave and leaves the choice to Poseidon. The novelist will clarify Theseus' motives at the beginning of *The Bull from the Sea*, but she has at least dispelled the idea that he acted either simplistically or ruthlessly. His ambivalent feelings for his father and his yearning for kingship prevented a rational decision. Thus Theseus slips into the sea, and as the waves close over him, he receives Poseidon's answer; or rather, he heard what he wanted to hear.

Designed as the companion piece to *The King Must Die*, *The Bull from the Sea* (1962) traces Theseus' fortunes from his triumphant return to Athens to his death on the island of Scyros (Skyros). Motifs which were of major importance in the first novel appear in miniature in the second. The first significant incident in *The King Must Die* was the sacrifice of the King Horse, who died "consenting." In the sequel, when Theseus arrives at Athens, he sacrifices a calf which also dies "consenting." There will also be a certain amount of recapitulation that is inevitable in a novel of this sort; Aegeus' death is summarized, and there are explanatory references to the Bull Court of Knossos, Theseus' first encounter with Phaedra, Ariadne's conversion to Dionysian worship on Naxos, and the revamping of the matriarchal society of Eleusis.

In one case, the recapitulation is an improvement over the original. Theseus' decision not to change the color of his sail was never fully explained at the end of *The King Must Die*. It seemed Mary Renault was trying to say that his dependence on Poseidon was often equivalent to a child's attempt to shift personal responsibility to a supernatural power. Theseus can lie to one of the barons and say that he simply forgot to hoist up the white sail, but he cannot deceive his old nurse. In a scene that seems to have been fashioned after the Odysseus-Eurycleia episode in the *Odyssey*, Theseus is so overcome by her awesome presence that he tells her everything.

The Theseus of tradition was forgetful, yet somehow a character's forgetfulness can compensate for the storyteller's lack of ingenuity. The device of "forgetting" is one of the oldest in literature, but it is usually reserved for melodrama where the incalculable is accepted as a

valid, if unimaginative, dénouement. Mary Renault's
Theseus is not the simplistic figure of myth; she has
given him considerably more complexity than he had in
any of his literary incarnations. If Theseus failed to
change the color of the sail, his reason would be rooted
in his ambivalent attitude toward his father. There is no
doubt that he resented Aegeus' never answering his request for aid to capture Crete. Furthermore, Theseus
is now ready to assume his kingship in Athens. But despite two excellent reasons for ignoring the pact he made
with his father, Theseus is also motivated by a vague
magnanimity: " 'I wanted to reach him before he knew
of my coming: to prove I came in peace, that I bore him
no ill will for failing me. . . . I prayed; and the god
sent me the sign I prayed for.' " [8] Torn between resentment and forgiveness, he left the choice to Poseidon.
One must infer that the sea whispered to him exactly
what he chose to hear.

Theseus is ready to be king, but *moira* never sanctions
human expectations before the fullness of time. In the
opening section of *The Bull from the Sea*, Mary Renault
has succeeded in defining artistically those bends in the
corridor of fate which everyone takes and which ultimately become one's destiny. Events that are seemingly
banal can, in the fullness of time, be the means of
achieving *moira*. Thus Theseus, who expects his kingship now, must still undergo another test. It will be a
degrading one, and necessarily so; in fact, it is almost
a perfect example of the New Testament paradox of
exaltation through humility.

Theseus must capture a Cretan bull called Podargos
that is loose on the plain of Marathon. To ensnare the
bull, he must repeat the ritual of the Bull Court. First
he must get a heifer to entice the bull; then he performs
the bull dance once more, not in the splendor of the
Minoan court, but on a plain. When Podargos is sacri-

ficed "consenting," Theseus knows from the paean that rises up to greet him that he is finally king.

In Gide's *Prometheus Misbound*, the hero still kept the vulture that gnawed at his liver while he was chained to a crag on Mount Caucasus. He is loath to part with this vestige of his former suffering, for the bird has now been transformed into a symbol of the agony (or masochism) which alone can produce art. Gradually the vulture was idealized; Prometheus kept it because its presence was a reminder of a time when life was at least not dull. The Bull Court to Theseus was much like the eagle of Gide's Prometheus. Barbaric and degrading as it was, the Bull Court afforded Theseus his greatest hour of glory, and with its absence he experienced the same kind of boredom that beset Tennyson's Ulysses while he sat idle on Ithaca. As the dying Thebe reminded Theseus, " 'There is nothing left like the Bull Court. No honor' " (p. 27).

Theseus misses the Bull Court and finds the unification of Attica a long and thankless task. He yearns for battle with its prospect of glory, and the bullring with the cheers and wagers. If Theseus were truly a king, he would fulfill the Platonic definition of the ideal man. Yet as a man, Theseus is severely limited. Unlike his son, Hippolytus (Hippolytos), who embodies the noblest ideals of Artemis and Apollo, Theseus is a human replica of Poseidon. He revels in his masculinity and is quick to throw off any form of female domination, proudly proclaiming " 'There is not much woman in me' " (p. 37). Although he has been in contact with royalty since he first witnessed the sacrifice of the King Horse, he has never learned the essential lesson of kingship: the subordination of personal desires to a higher good. All that is required to bring out his restlessness is the appearance of the roving Pirithous (Pirithoos), and like Tennyson's Ulysses, he is ready "to seek a newer world."

It is Theseus' two-fisted masculinity that endears him to Pirithous, and it is in their mutual need for male companionship that their friendship consists. The model is again Homeric; the men begin by trading insults and end by exchanging daggers. Mary Renault clearly had in mind the encounter between Glaucus and Diomedes in the *Iliad* where the two warriors, one a Trojan and the other a Greek, renounced their enmity and proclaimed their lasting friendship by an exchange of armor.

With Pirithous, Theseus embarks on a series of exploits that take him to the southeastern shores of the Black Sea and the land of the Amazons. The famed Calydonian Boar Hunt is not described in detail; the author assumes an acquaintance with it, or at least with Swinburne's *Atalanta in Calydon*. "A fine boar-hunt we had there" (p. 52) sums up the incident, and those who know the myth will interpret the statement, "as happens often, the best man died," as a reference to the ill-starred Meleager.

The journey to the Centaurs is one of the most impressive sections in the novel. By modern standards, Centaurs belong to the realm of *Märchen* and hardly seem worthy of artistic treatment. Except for some of the Elgin Marbles which show Lapiths and Centaurs in combat or Piero di Cosimo's painting on the same subject, the plight of these mythological creatures seems only able to evoke pathos. Even John Updike's *The Centaur*, in which the Chiron of myth assumes the form of a high-school teacher, is little more than a sentimental tribute to the author's Pennsylvania boyhood where everyone, including the postmistress, has a mythological equivalent.

In Greek myth, the Centaurs appeared as a wild and boisterous tribe whose interests centered exclusively about wine, brawls, and rape. Chiron alone was different from his fellows. Renowned for his wisdom and gentleness, he was always depicted as a tutor who could proudly number Asclepius, Jason, and Achilles among his students. Wounded by one of Hercules' poisoned arrows, he was unable to bear the pain and achieved death by offering his immortality to Prometheus.

Mary Renault knows the legend of Chiron well, but in her treatment of it there is no room for the obvious. First of all, the name of Chiron is never used; instead one reads about a gentle Centaur called "Old Handy." The initiated will know that "Chiron" comes from the Greek noun for "hand" (*cheir*). "Old Handy" is the author's way of adding a new dimension to the myth as well as having a bit of linguistic fun with the classically educated.

At times Mary Renault's mythopoetic art cannot be separated from the scientific method she learned during her years as a nurse. In her portrait of Chiron she chose to emphasize the Centaur as physician in contradistinction to Updike who stressed the Centaur as teacher. When Old Handy bends over a sick Centaur baby or squats down at the side of Pirithous' aged father, the language assumes a stark objectivity that refuses to surrender its tautness to sentimentality. The tenderness which Old Handy exhibits as he makes his rounds represents the transfiguration of the hospital world and suggests that the deformed and lonely Centaur learned the lesson of humanity that the sisters of the early novels never acquired from their daily prayers in chapel.

Theseus must next come in contact with Oedipus. Their meeting is one of the most important features of the myth, and it occurs in Sophocles' *Oedipus at Colonnus* and in Gide's *Theseus*. Traditionally, Theseus befriended Oedipus at Colonnus (about a mile northwest of Athens) and was also present at his death. While their confrontation is *de rigueur* for any author dealing with this myth (unless he is aiming at pure symbolism like Kazantzakis in *Kouros*), Mary Renault is not so much influenced by literary precedent as she is by her theory of kingship. Her Theseus is a king who is not yet a priest, and it is fitting that he should encounter a true priest-king.

Colonnus is earthquake-ridden, and Theseus goes there to offer a sacrifice at the neglected shrine of Poseidon. The mention of Colonnus should prepare the knowing reader for the inevitable meeting of Theseus and Oedipus. First the novelist gives a few salient details; a man whose feet were "warped like the wood of a tree which had been spiked as a sapling" (p. 65) is being stoned by angry villagers. The victim of their rage is Oedipus, who is accompanied by his daughter Antigone.

Like so many episodes in Mary Renault's Greek novels, the meeting with Oedipus combines literary criticism with characterization. The sophomoric view of *Oedipus the King* as a drama of predestination fortunately ended with Francis Fergusson's *The Idea of a Theater* which viewed the Sophoclean tragedy as a detective story in which the object of the investigation became the subject, or as the novelist's Oedipus says, " 'So I began to seek step after step into the darkness, on the path that led me to myself' " (p. 69).

Mary Renault clearly intended Oedipus to be an *exemplum* for Theseus. Initially Oedipus does not seem to be too different from Theseus, for he also yearned for an easy way out of the labyrinth of destiny. When the plague struck Thebes, Oedipus was certain his sacrificial death would save the city. He had hoped the oracle would require that "the king must die," but learned instead that the murder of Laius must first be avenged. In his quest for the murderer of Laius, Oedipus learned of his past and experienced perfect self-knowledge.

Unlike Theseus, Oedipus is also a priest who performs

one last sacrificial act—the giving up of his life. He recalls a dream-vision in which Apollo appeared to him and asked who he was. Oedipus, who solved the riddle of the Sphinx with the word "Man," gives the same response to the god: " 'My lord—only a man' " (p. 70). His answer is now stripped of anything hybristic; it is the response of someone at the moment of "consenting."

According to myth, Oedipus passed from life in a mysterious way. A peal of thunder announced that his end was near, and Theseus led him to the place of his death. But Mary Renault will have none of the supernatural. Her Oedipus disappears in an earthquake which Theseus knew would occur and in which he thought he too would die. However, *moira* bypassed Theseus and claimed only Oedipus.

It is the contemporary author's privilege to alter a myth, but Mary Renault's ingenious retelling of the murder of Laius at the crossroads loses much of its power because Oedipus recounts the incident himself. Yet it contains the germ of a brilliant idea on which some future novelist might elaborate—Jocasta's presence in the carriage at the time of her husband's murder. In *The Bull from the Sea*, not only does Oedipus slay Laius and his entourage, but he also drags Jocasta from the carriage and hurls her across her husband's body. That Oedipus would marry the one witness to the murder may seem to be carrying irony to the limit, yet children of fortune will dare the outrageous. As for Jocasta: " 'She had only seen me in my anger; blood and rage and the grime of the dusty road will change a man. She was not sure' " (p. 74).

Oedipus was a *tyrannos*, a word which does not necessarily connote a wicked ruler but rather someone who managed to obtain sole power in a state—an autocrat in the modern sense. But Oedipus was not a natural king, for his kingship was acquired when he assumed control of Thebes after Laius' death. The next "king" Theseus will meet will be one who was born to the role, Hippolyta, Queen of the Amazons.

Because the Amazons emulated male warriors, they regarded Hippolyta as their "king." Theseus is also of royal stock, but when he sets sail for Pontus and a new adventure, "the king . . . was on holiday" (p. 87). Although he is now a rover, he will learn from this new king, for the author has wisely set up the books of Marathon and Pontus as a diptych where two forms of kingship, political and natural, are contrasted.

The Amazon episode is one of the novelist's most sensuous pieces of description. From the opening picture of women with "breasts as perfect as wine cups" (p. 93) to the tragic death of Hippolyta in Theseus' arms, the reader is experiencing the author's great gift for the depiction of passion. There was an undercurrent of sensuality in *The Last of the Wine*, particularly in the idyllic encounter between Alexias and Lysis; but it was only a moment in their relationship and a minor part of the book. But in *The King Must Die* and *The Bull from the Sea*, Theseus' sexual nature necessitates a masculine approach to everything he does, and Mary Renault imparts a pulsating virility to all of his actions.

His first glimpse of Hippolyta on horseback is one of the author's most successful pieces of iconography and recalls the friezelike description of Julian Fleming in *Return to Night*. When Theseus falls in love with Hippolyta at first sight, it is not because of her beauty, remarkable as it is; rather it is a love that can only exist between equals, between two kings: " 'She is more than queen. She understands the sacrifice that goes consenting. There is a king's fate in her eyes' " (p. 101).

Mary Renault has their relationship begin with an archetypal act—the hero's invasion of a female ritual which should, under ordinary circumstances, result in his death. But this is not the first time Theseus was in a situation where he profaned a rite sacred to women; his subconscious fear of female domination and his desire to replace matrilinear societies with patrilinear ones partially explain his excessively masculine nature. Because he has witnessed what he should not, Theseus must fight Hippolyta in single combat. The format will again be Homeric—the introductions, genealogy, and the oath by the river Styx. The fight is more than a battle of the sexes. Mary Renault has already described Hippolyta in animal imagery, and the epithet "leopard" is a recurrent one. It is really a battle of kings, one untamed and so feline in her movements that she will become a "little leopard" to her new husband; the other so conscious that he is subduing a woman that he acts as if it were a rape. The scene ends with Hippolyta's submission, and as a fitting coda, a threnody goes up from the Amazons.

Hippolyta is the ideal mate for Theseus—a king for a king. The brief life they have together fulfills the Platonic dream that Leo Lane of *The Middle Mist* envisioned for herself—"a man with his friend." Hippolyta is also the perfect *philos,* for she can supply the companionship in battle that Theseus formerly required of Pirithous. While Theseus rightly insists he is not a lover of boys, he has a relationship with Hippolyta which could only have been realized with a male companion, except for the heterosexual gratification that they experience after a day of high adventure. In a sense, he achieved the Greek goal of bisexuality with a female lover who was also a "friend." Their life together was one of two warriors sharing exploits and desires: "We learned as much of each other in battle as we did in bed" (p. 122).

In myth, little mention is made of Hippolyta (sometimes called Antiope) except for the fact that she died during an Amazon invasion of Athens. Mary Renault will include a similar invasion, but her rationalism forbids anything so fanciful as an Amazon war. According to popular etymology, Amazon means "breast-less," but the novelist prefers to follow Robert Graves who argues for a derivation from the Armenian word for moon-women.[9] Thus the Amazons of legend become the Moon Maids of Artemis, a sensible transformation, for it accounts for Hippolyta's devotion to the virgin goddess as well as for her son's chastity. The Amazons will also form the vanguard of a Scythian invasion of Athens—a learned touch on the author's part, for there is support from Herodotus for such a joint attack.

Hippolyta will die in the invasion, but with a typical Mary Renault twist. " 'But fate never comes in the shape men look for' " (p. 156) Theseus comments, little knowing that his next bout with *moira* will also fall short of his expectations. An oracle requires a sacrifice to stop the Scythian horde. Theseus thinks he will be that sacrifice and that by his death he will become the subject of epic. He therefore "consents," but Hippolyta intercepts the arrow intended for him and unwittingly robs him of his *kudos*.

In Hippolyta's death, Theseus has witnessed the ultimate act of kingship—one king's offering his life for another. Since Hippolyta was a king, it is fitting that her body should be carried on a shield by the young men of her guard. It is equally fitting that Theseus' final recollection of her should be as a king: "But the King had been called; and the King had died" (p. 188).

Hippolytus has always presented a problem for the mythmaker, particularly since he only seems to be suffering from what Auden called "the distortions of ingrown virginity." In an effort to explain his asceticism, Mary Renault adds a touch of anachronistic Christianity to the myth. One must remember that Theseus allowed

Hippolytus to be named after his mother despite the resentment that would come from an antimatriarchal society. Since Hippolyta was a priestess of Artemis, her son would naturally grow in devotion to the goddess. When the seven-year-old boy is discovered on the palace roof in a trancelike state, the reader may begin to suspect that the model for Hippolytus is not entirely Euripidean. " 'I was with the Lady' " (p. 158) was the boy's reply to his frightened parents. Christ gave a similarly nonchalant answer to Mary and Joseph when they asked him where he had been for three days in Jerusalem: "How is it that you sought me? Did you not know that I must be about my Father's business?" (Luke 2:49–50).

Mary Renault's Hippolytus is a Christ figure who transforms his devotion to Artemis into a vow of chastity. Blessed with the gift of healing, he prefigures the Christian ideal of the king-physician-priest and embodies the qualities usually associated with Jesus Christ under the titles of High Priest and Healer of Souls.

Dramatically, Hippolytus stands in sharp contrast to his father. While Theseus was endowed with an earthquake aura, Hippolytus has the gift of healing. Hippolytus' gifts, both natural and divine, differ from his father's. The boy is a virgin at seventeen while Theseus boasts of having sired children at that age. Hippolytus possesses the height his father always craved. As a youth, Theseus was the Kouros of Poseidon, while his son is nicknamed the Kouros of the Maiden.

Hippolytus completes the one-sided masculinity of his father. Theseus modeled himself after Poseidon and vigorously avoided any contact with the more civilized Olympians, particularly the goddesses. The key to Theseus' aggressive masculinity can be found in the famous statue of Poseidon in the National Museum in Athens. Everything about the statue is larger than life; the arms are defiantly outstretched, and the body is poised for hurling the trident. A face of self-satisfied virility is framed by a flowing beard with ringlets of hair symmetrically adorning the brow. Such was the goal to which Theseus aspired—a body which proclaimed its indomitable masculinity.

Hippolytus, on the other hand, did not limit himself to one deity; he worshipped the virgin huntress Artemis and her brother Apollo, god of the civilizing arts such as poetry and medicine. Because Hippolytus is a mystic who has transcended the flesh, his relationship with his stepmother Phaedra becomes the perennial *agon* between the ascetic and the sensualist. Like Theseus, Phaedra has a one-sided sexual nature; she possesses the lust of her mother Pasiphae and has little in common with Hippolyta who was the perfect female (wife-friend). Since most versions of the Hippolytus myth are in the form of plays, Phaedra's attraction to her stepson is almost instantaneous. But the novel is a less restricted medium and allows for greater freedom and originality in the unfolding of the plot and the awakening of desire.

Thus Mary Renault's Phaedra is at first cool to Hippolytus, for she has a son of her own by Theseus, Acamas (Akamas), whom she would naturally want to inherit the throne. Soon there is a marked change in her. After her initiation into the Eleusinian Mysteries, Phaedra faints as a raven encircles Hippolytus' head. She then complains of chronic headaches, and Hippolytus is sent to cure them. In the course of his visits, she confesses her lust to him; bound in conscience never to reveal it, Hippolytus must be silent when Phaedra falsely accuses him of rape.

Theseus' curse is the stuff of which melodrama is made, yet the author cannot alter tradition so radically as to reject it, particularly in view of the title she has given her novel. The Euripidean Theseus used his last curse against his son. Hippolytus left Troezen, and as he went along the coast, a tidal wave with a bull springing from its crest rolled toward the shore, frightened the horses, and caused the chariot to overturn. Hippolytus was left with barely enough life for a reconciliation with his repentant father.

In the novel, Hippolytus' death also occurred in Troezen where he went as his grandfather's heir and where Phaedra persuaded Theseus to take her on the pretext of seeing Acamas. True to tradition, father curses son, but the curse takes the form of an earthquake. Thus Theseus has used his gift to destroy Hippolytus. The bull also appears, coming forth on the wave and symbolizing Poseidon's powerful wrath. But one should also think back to book one where the old nurse warned Theseus to " 'loose not the Bull from the Sea' " (p. 10). At the time he thought it was the Cretan bull that had escaped on the plain of Marathon. Thus the old woman's prophecy was really a form of dramatic foreshadowing.

In book five, Theseus' recollections become hazy. This brief, sparsely written chapter brings the remembrance to a close. After the death of Hippolytus, the Theseus of myth abducted Helen of Troy, kidnapped Persephone and made a fruitless descent to the underworld to bring back Pirithous. The Theseus of Mary Renault, a middle-aged man suffering from a stroke that left him paralyzed on one side, scoffs at the legends that have grown up around him. The Theseus of myth was also murdered on the rocky island of Scyros by King Lycomedes (Lykomedes). But Mary Renault's Lycomedes harbors no such purpose: " 'If my house speaks of home to you, so use it' " (p. 267).

Theseus interprets his host's welcome as an invitation to fulfill his *moira*. Choosing a crag from which a man could accidentally fall, he leaps to his death like his father before him. To the literal-minded, Theseus' death would be suicide, but that is not the author's final observation on the life of her hero. On the previous night he dreamt he was a young man again; yet when he woke, there were no regrets that what had passed was only a dream. Now he has the courage to die, for there can be no further adventures for a paralytic. Death will insure his immortality; he will not be remembered as Theseus of the limping foot but as Theseus the slayer of the Minotaur. As he falls to the sea below, it is not with the crash of a suicide but with the grace of a youthful swimmer "plunging with the dolphins" (p. 268).

Peter Wolfe maintains that *The Bull from the Sea* is Mary Renault's weakest novel since *The Middle Mist*. He is probably correct; reading it is comparable to peering into a kaleidoscope and watching flashes of light and color which stun by their chaotic iridescence. What is so fascinating about the novel is the episodic, almost Herodotean structure where the author's insights into well-known myths leave one with the feeling that he has witnessed an act of mythopoesis, but not necessarily an act of fiction. Still, *The Bull from the Sea* is filled with ingenious touches—Jocasta's presence at the murder of her husband; Chiron (Old Handy) as a physician-teacher; the progression of king figures (Oedipus, Hippolyta, Hippolytus), each of whom teaches Theseus something about the nature of a ruler; Hippolytus as Christ figure; an Amazon world reconstructed not as a society of breastless warriors but as a lost Eden which Theseus and his men invade. All of these innovations force the reader to rethink his schoolbook mythology and answer the question that is always latent in myth: What is one left with when the layers of legendary accretions are stripped away? And the answer would seem to be: human beings with perennially human motives and desires.

Consider Mary Renault's solution to the Hippolytus-Phaedra-Theseus triangle. In the classical versions (Euripides and Seneca), Phaedra's passion for her stepson had begun before the play opens. In *The Bull from the Sea*, Phaedra progresses from initial coolness to overt lust. In Euripides, Theseus is merely a stock father-tyrant who sends his errant son into exile. One gathers that Theseus loved Phaedra and looked upon her dishonor as a personal disgrace. Yet when he learned the truth, he could only bewail his son's untimely death.

Mary Renault severely criticizes the Euripidean account. She assumes, and rightly so, that Theseus' one great love was Hippolyta. Why else would he allow his son to be named after her? His marriage to Phaedra was prompted by political expediency and nothing more. Thus his reaction to Phaedra's accusation is considerably more complex than it was in Euripides. The novelist's Theseus is a highly sexed male conscious of his virility and expounding it as if it were a philosophy of life. Hippolytus is completely different. When he refuses to betray Phaedra's secret, Theseus cries: " 'Some god hold me back, before I take this little man and break him between my hands' " (p. 238). Yet it is Theseus who is the "little man" and Hippolytus who possesses stature.

Traditionally, Theseus' curse was triggered by Phaedra's incriminating letter. In the novel, Theseus was also infuriated by his wife's alleged rape, but what preyed on his mind was the fact that Hippolytus had stepped out of his role of celibate. Theseus' realization that he has been misled plays havoc with his imagination and evokes an image of Ariadne covered with blood and wine. Ariadne, the priestess of the Mother Goddess, sank to bestiality, and now his son also seems to be reversing roles.

Mary Renault asks one final question about the

myth: Would Phaedra really have committed suicide after Hippolytus spurned her? If vengeance were her motive, self-destruction, while theatrically effective, would rob her disclosure of all its perverse drama. A note tied to a wrist is no substitute for a grandiloquent speech of betrayal. In the novel, Phaedra tells Theseus that his son had ravished her. When Theseus learns the truth from Acamas, he acts in perfect accord with his character as the novelist has defined it. The man who killed Procrustes, struck Molpadia dead without even realizing it, and slew both Minos and Asterion, would react in one way; he would murder Phaedra and make her death seem a suicide.

4

The Gathering Dusk: *The Mask of Apollo*

Anyone reading Mary Renault's Greek novels in their order of publication will probably be dismayed at the bald, angular style of *The Mask of Apollo* (1966). A decade had elapsed between her first and second attempts at historical fiction; in the interim she wrote the Theseus books which, strictly speaking, are legendary romance. For *The King Must Die*, she found a style that was epithetic enough to sound Homeric; it was grandiose and simile-laden, while *The Last of the Wine* was pure Attic. Since Mary Renault spent a decade examining two different aspects of Greek civilization (the historical and the mythological), she was naturally unable to work in one style. The tension involved in duplicating two radically distinct styles in English, the Attic and the Homeric, can even be seen in *The Bull from the Sea* where the author seemed unable to repeat the poetically archaic language of *The King Must Die*.

The Mask of Apollo is also not without stylistic infelicities; one reason is the first person narration by Nikoteros (Niko), an actor who, like others in his profession, speaks the words of literary masters but never achieves a similar art in writing his memoirs. Still, one might argue that Niko's (and the author's) disillusionment with fourth-century Greece which drapes the events in crepuscular folds can only find a voice in language that has been stripped of every refinement.

Regardless, *The Mask of Apollo* is Mary Renault's most ambitious novel, for it attempts tragedy on three levels —cultural, philosophical, and political. It interweaves the decline of the theatre with Plato's inability to apply his philosophy to the real world and Dion's failure to establish a constitutional monarchy in Syracuse headed by a philosopher-king.

The theatre has always been a minor theme in Mary Renault's fiction; usually it symbolized a retreat from the restrictions of the hospital world. Julian Fleming's (*Return to Night*) interest in costumes and makeup would brand him as effeminate in contemporary society; but in Greece where men assumed the female roles in the drama, an actor like Niko, whose father excelled at playing women's roles, would feel neither shame nor isolation. For Niko, the theatre is not a place of withdrawal but a temple where the mysteries of life and death are celebrated. Thus *The Mask of Apollo* replaces the earlier theme of Theatre as Asylum with Theatre as Temple where the limitations of gender give way to the exigencies of art.

Like *The Last of the Wine*, *The Mask of Apollo* is also a memoir; the audience for whom it was intended is unimportant, for it is primarily Niko's attempt to place his life and his profession within a historical context. The first chapter in which the narrator reconstructs his youth follows the familiar lines of *The Last of the Wine* and *The King Must Die*. Niko recalls playing one of Medea's sons at the age of three; at six he almost ruined a performance of Euripides' *The Trojan Women* when, as the dead Astyanax, he began to sob during Hecuba's lament. When Niko was nineteen, his father died. His dilemma is almost proverbial: "Boys left like me have had to choose between selling their favors to some actor in return for work, or going right to the bottom." [1] Since "the glory that was Greece" is now only a memory, Niko is forced to join Lamprias' touring company with its actors who relive past triumphs and resort to bitchery when they find themselves eclipsed by younger talent.

The reader who is dismayed by Mary Renault's treatment of the decline of the theatre should remember that the fourth century was more famous for great actors than for great playwrights. Furthermore, the Golden Age of Greek Drama was rather short-lived; it lasted half a century at most. Even Aristophanes knew it had passed; in *The Frogs* (405 B.C.), he argued that Aeschylus alone should return to earth and restore the theatre to its pride of place. Handbooks and Classical Civilization courses have a tendency to group the three major tragedians together as monuments of the Periclean Age. However, to Socrates, and later to Nietzsche, Euripides was *sui generis*; it was he who took the theatre from its sacred niche and anchored it in the soil of reality by subjecting the gods to ridicule and substituting human passions for abstract themes. Both philosophers felt that Euripides destroyed the theatre's exalted position, although few scholars today would accept their verdict. Certainly some of Euripides' later plays (*Ion, Helen, Iphigenia in Tauris*) approximate the extravagances of melodrama with their recognition scenes and happy endings; in some respects they signal the advent of New Comedy with its stock characters and situations. Ironically, in *The Birth of Tragedy*, Nietzsche attributed the death of the drama to Socrates and his quest for definition which succeeded in destroying myth; but he was no less harsh to Euripides who, in his opinion, transported the common man from the auditorium to the stage.

Niko, who is heir to a tradition where the drama made men seem better than they were, has entered a profession that is considerably less noble than it was in his father's day. When the oligarchs interrupt a performance at a small town near Olympia, Niko saves the day by declaiming a speech from Aeschylus' *The Persians* while wearing the mask of Apollo. The mask which is half a century old symbolizes the theatre of his father's time; Niko's identification with the mask represents the dream of man's nobility on which the drama of the Periclean Age was founded. His conversations with the mask hark back to Theseus' dialogues with Poseidon; both men owe their powers to an Olympian, but to Niko the god is a symbol of artistic achievement rather than a convenient object of prayer in time of need.

After the first chapter in which an inglorious present is juxtaposed against a fabled past, the novel moves into history. In *The Last of the Wine*, the fictitious characters, Alexias and Lysis, walked alongside historical figures like Plato and Socrates. Niko is also an invented character, although his name was probably suggested by Nicostratos who was admired in antiquity for his excellent delivery of messenger-speeches. Niko's career will become a transversal bisecting two parallel actions: Dion's dream of transforming his native Syracuse into an aristocracy and Plato's attempt to educate Dionysius II according to the program he outlined in the *Republic*. Niko's entry into Dion's circle occurs with the utmost naturalness. At twenty-six, he is a respected actor performing in Aeschylus' now lost tragedy, *The Myrmidons*, at Delphi. After the performance which almost culminated in disaster through the machinations of a jealous actor, Niko receives an unknown admirer backstage who invites him to dinner that evening. The stranger speaks with such imperial civility that one cannot doubt his importance in the novel: " 'I will send my servant for you. . . . My name is Dion, a citizen of Syracuse' " (p. 44).

In none of her novels has the author asked more of her readers. To all but the specialist, the history of fourth-century Greece is an intricate web of tyrannies and despotisms. Yet the tragedy of Dion whose noble aspirations buckled under the weight of corruption (significantly, Plutarch pairs him with Brutus in the *Parallel Lives*) is understandable only in terms of history.

Dion (ca. 408–354 B.C.) was the minister and brother-in-law of Dionysius I, tyrant of Syracuse. Dionysius married Dion's sister, Aristomache, and Dion himself wed one of the daughters of that marriage, Arete, his own niece; thus Dion became Dionysius' son-in-law as well. Dionysius I does not appear in *The Mask of Apollo*, but Niko feels his influence everywhere; not only is he asked to appear in his play, *Hector's Ransoming*, but after the tyrant's death, he is also requested to deliver the funeral oration in Syracuse.

To Aristotle, Dionysius I was a demagogic tyrant and little more than a warlord, but modern historians view him in a different light. While his tyranny lasted for thirty-eight years and was completely unconstitutional, he bound his empire with "chains of adamant" by a strong army and navy, and turned Ortygia into a fortified residence which could only be entered through five successive gates. He made Syracuse the leading city of Sicily and a continental power as well; but his greatest achievement consisted in saving Sicily from complete domination by Carthage, which after four wars still held a third of the island.

Dionysius also fancied himself a playwright, although the comic poets often ridiculed his efforts. It seems that he purchased Aeschylus' desk and Euripides' harp, neither of which inspired him very much. He dreamed of winning first prize in the dramatic festivals, and in 367 B.C. his play, *Hector's Ransoming*, won at the Lenaea. The tyrant became so elated that he died from excessive celebration.

With the accession of Dionysius II, the idealistic Dion believed he could rid Syracuse of tyranny by introducing a constitution modeled after Plato's *Republic*. Plato had come to Sicily in 388 B.C. at the request of the elder Dionysius, only to be sold into slavery at Aegina because of his open criticism of Syracusan luxury; now he would make a second visit (361 B.C.) to mold the tyrant's son into a philosopher-king.

In the novel, Niko first sees the incipient philosopher-king playing with toy chariots. Mary Renault has assimilated Plutarch's *Life of Dion*; according to the historian, the elder Dionysius, fearing his son might someday gain power over him, kept him closely guarded at home where he occupied his time making small wagons, lampstands, chairs, and tables. Apart from his penchant for carpentry, Dionysius II is even more ill-equipped for kingship; one of the cardinal virtues of Platonism is temperance, but the young Dionysius would have difficulty acquiring it if he persisted in staging orgies that lasted for ninety consecutive days.

Dionysius II could only have been Dion's ideal of a constitutional monarch. After Niko saw him in his mindless splendor, he reflected: "Neither of us . . . is perfect casting for a philosophic king. I'm the lucky one; I need not try" (p. 118.) It is difficult to imagine Plato's even considering a return visit to Sicily, particularly in view of the treatment he received at the hands of Dionysius I. In the *Seventh Epistle*, Plato made it clear that the reason for his second voyage was to dispel the widespread belief that he was only a theorist whose philosophy had no practical application. Mary Renault's Plato is also eager to put his theory into practice: " 'But one does not want to end by finding one has been only a thing of words' " (p. 124). There was also Plato's great love for Dion, who was his best student during his first stay in Syracuse. From the poem which Mary Renault uses as the epigraph for *The Mask of Apollo*, it is clear that the philosopher could never shatter Dion's grand illusion.

The novel vividly dramatizes Plato's second Sicilian

visit and suggests two reasons for its failure, both of which can be corroborated by history. Plato, who would not dilute his theories even for an intractable subject, began the tyrant's education with the study of geometry which the impressionable youth undertook with short-lived enthusiasm. More important, Plutarch has suggested that Dionysius harbored a neurotic love for Plato; like a tenacious student who would not share his favorite teacher with other pupils, Dionysius was jealous of the esteem in which Plato held Dion. Mary Renault leaves no doubt that Dionysius' conversion to philosophy was motivated by passion: " 'Youth worships the mask of love; that is his [Dionysius'] Eros, a powerful god' " (p. 145).

Dion is banished presumably because of a letter he sent the Carthaginians, asking them to insist upon his presence at any peace conference with Syracuse. Niko hears the news of the banishment immediately after he has performed Euripides' *Bacchae*. In the course of the performance, he noticed to his horror that the actor playing Pentheus was wearing a mask that had an uncanny resemblance to Dion. Euripides' tragedy depicting the unresolved struggle between emotion and reason becomes a metaphor for Syracuse itself which, like Pentheus' Thebes, suffered from a similar polarization— the irrational Dionysius who was easy prey to envy and rumor vs. the philosophical Dion who yearned only for an ideal state. Although Dion's indiscreet letter to Carthage was the alleged reason for his banishment, one cannot help but think that Dionysius' jealousy of his friendship with Plato was the decisive factor. Paralleling Dionysius' fanatical passion for Plato was Niko's spiritual love for Dion which represented true *philia*: "I knew I had met a man I would gladly die for" (p. 57). Niko was only a peripheral member of Plato's Academy, but as an artist dealing in truth cloaked by illusion, he understood Winged Eros without the promptings of the master philosopher.

In one of the novel's finest episodes which shows the author's extraordinary power of expressing philosophical ideas in terms congenial to fiction, Niko confronts Dionysius after he has been exposed to Plato's views on art as imitation. Since Plato has oversimplified his ideas on art in the *Republic*, Dionysius has no trouble assimilating them and proceeds to rehash all the arguments for Niko's benefit: poets depict ignoble and unstable men; they portray the baser emotions of grief and despair; their effect on young minds is pernicious.

Even the most confirmed Platonists have difficulty reconciling Plato's pejorative view of literature with his own art which is so intensely literary that when Niko first hears a passage from the *Phaedo*, he asks from which play it was taken. Mary Renault also realizes that Plato's ban on poets constitutes something of a blight on his philosophy. In the Author's Note, she cautions that "Plato's concern about the contents of plays should, in fairness, be seen not as a mere censorship of ideas, but more like the wish of an enlightened Christian to drop from the liturgy passages about the wicked gnashing their teeth in flames of eternal torment" (p. 325).[2] Consequently, she has Speusippus (Speusippos) tell Niko: " '*The Republic* is . . . a discussion of principles, not a working code. . . . I think the purpose of those passages was to startle our poets into responsibility' " (p. 161).

Apart from its splendid transformation of philosophy into drama, the episode is important for another reason: it pits the artist's point of view against the critic's. Ancient, unlike modern, literary criticism was written for the most part by philosophers, orators, and rhetoricians—Plato, Aristotle, Longinus, Cicero, Quintilian—and not by poets, dramatists or artists. The sole exception is Horace, but the *Ars Poetica* never touches his forte, the lyric, but concerns itself exclusively with epic and drama. One can only deduce Sophocles' theory of tragedy from his extant plays and Horace's concept of lyric from his poetry. When Niko defends himself against the charge that actors portray base characters, he is reiterating the time-honored credo that art transcends morality and that there is a difference between openly endorsing evil and merely using it within a dramatic context—a point that Plato for all his dialectical skill failed to make.

In *The Last of the Wine*, Mary Renault paid Socrates the homage which he customarily receives. Since she could find no fault with him, he remained a nebulous figure, omnipresent but disembodied. Her Dion is another matter; more fallible than Socrates, he is also more human as a literary creation. Dion becomes tragic man, and he knows it; like the other characters in the novel who resort to playacting to retain the dignity that their culture has abandoned, Dion assumes the part of the man without a country and plays it for sheer pathos, despite the fact that during his nine-year exile he lacked neither comforts nor companions.

Yet Dion is not beyond reproach; because Mary Renault emphasizes his weaknesses as well as his virtues, he becomes a tragic figure in a way Socrates never was. The tragic hero's fall from eminence occurs through some error in judgment or moral flaw. Dion's uncompromising nature could easily be mistaken for hybris; consequently, many of his friends distrusted him and believed that if he ever succeeded in deposing Dionysius, he would rule Syracuse himself. At the end of his *Fourth Epistle*, Plato warned Dion in veiled language not to adopt too severe an attitude toward his fellow Syracusans: "Remember that some think you are not compliant enough; a spirit of accommodation is necessary if you would accomplish anything among men, but *hauteur* has only solitude for company."

When Dionysius invited Plato to make another visit to Syracuse, Dion encouraged his friend, thinking undoubtedly of his own interests. Plutarch states that Dionysius would show no mercy to Dion unless Plato returned to his court. While Plato made his third visit to Sicily at the age of seventy and in a state of poor health, his chief motive could only have been to effect Dion's recall and to reconcile him with Dionysius. It is impossible to believe that Plato paid any heed to the reports that Dionysius was making progress in philosophy, although he might have been curious about the rumor that the tyrant had made a compendium of his doctrines. But Plato is also playing a role—the disillusioned intellectual in the twilight of his life, trying to intercede for Dion as he never could for Socrates. Before Plato set sail for Syracuse, he and Dion "exchanged a ceremonial kiss, like two kings in tragedy" (p. 214). It is as if immersion in their roles had reduced them to uncorporeal essences as they were about to make the transition from living history to deathless legend.

While Plato remained Dion's friend to the last, Niko soon became disenchanted with him. After he learned that Dion endorsed Plato's views on the drama, the idolatry vanished; Niko no longer saw Dion's face, but rather a mask. The person of Dion had metamorphosed into the mask of tragedy, and all that remained of the man was the face of a suffering king.

Historically, Mary Renault is correct in her characterization of Dion. While no one can doubt that Dion's commitment to the *Republic* was genuine, he was greatly handicapped by his kinship with tyrants and his association with Plato whom many Syracusans regarded with contempt and considered little more than a sophist. It is also difficult to imagine how a man whom Plutarch

called a "consummate general" could have been out-
stripped by Heraclides (Herakleides). Even more dis-
concerting is Dion's implication in Heraclides' murder
which suggests that he became a tyrant in spite of himself. Perhaps Dion's greatest error was his inability to
distinguish between his friends and his enemies. At the
end of the *Seventh Epistle*, which is both a panegyric to
Dion and an *apologia pro vita sua*, Plato contends that
Dion really never understood the nature of the men who
finally killed him and thus failed to take precautions
against them.

Every tragedy has its overtones of irony; in 354 B.C.
Dion was murdered by the order of Callippus
(Kallippos), one of his most trusted supporters and a
former member of Plato's Academy. Every tragedy also
has its portentous moments. Plutarch relates that shortly
before he was slain, Dion had a vision of a Fury sweeping
out his house with a broom. The novelist also records
the apparition but emphasizes its masklike face. The last
thrust of the knife is that Dion, whose attempt at political reform alienated his own people and brought war to
his own city, should experience a portent usually reserved for the damned.

While *The Mask of Apollo* deals with one of the most
tragic periods in ancient history, it does not end with a
stifled cry of anguish; rather it closes on a note of historical inevitability. The decline of Athens was paralleled
by the rise of Rome; in the character of Rupilius, one
sees the Roman practicality that was to inject a new life
into the Mediterranean world. When Rupilius contrasts
the two civilizations, one can almost hear Anchises
telling Aeneas how the Hellenic superiority in the arts
will be counterbalanced by Rome's military achievements.

Hellas was destined for one final moment of glory;
significantly the novel which shuttled back and forth

between Greece and Sicily terminates at Pella where Niko is to perform Aeschylus' *The Myrmidons* once more. His protégé, Thettalos, has encouraged him to don the mask of Achilles, although Niko feels he is too old for the part. But the reason for Thettalos' insistence is that he has become enamored of a youth of Pella whom he regards with the same awe that Niko once had for Dion. The youth has a particular affinity for the *Iliad*, most of which he has memorized; he also identifies with Achilles, and like Homer's hero, he has his own Patroclus. The young man is, of course, Alexander the Great; and the fact that the novel ends at Pella where his father had his great palace suggests that the annals of Hellas have not been irrevocably closed.

At the end of *The Bull from the Sea*, Achilles was also on the island of Scyros when Theseus plunged to his death. His presence there indicated that new heroes always replace the old as if in some preordained cycle. Alexander's brief appearance at the end of *The Mask of Apollo* suggests that new life will come forth from the corpse of an exhausted civilization. *The Myrmidons*, in which Aeschylus portrayed Patroclus and Achilles as lover and beloved, represented the ideal relationship for Niko; but it was one that seemed unrealizable on earth. Unlike the *Phaedrus* in *The Charioteer* which set an unattainable goal for the characters, *The Myrmidons* becomes the dream fulfilled, for Alexander and his lover Hephaestion (Hephaistion) will enact the parts of Achilles and Patroclus, if only for a fleeting moment in history.

Art alone survives power struggles and the vain quest for ideal systems. It is the only legacy that one age can bequeath to another. Of all the characters in the novel, Niko alone escapes despair. While the decline of the theatre is a personal loss for him, he never really becomes a tragic figure; the mask of Apollo and the

Socratic philosophy of "Be what you want to *seem*" have enabled him to invest his art with an Aeschylean grandeur, although the Golden Age of the drama has long since passed.

Niko acts as if verisimilitude still has a place on the stage. Neither Dion nor Plato can achieve the vicarious dignity that art brings, for they have rejected it as an inferior imitation of the real. Dion's tragedy was that of the idealist who pursued one course of action to the exclusion of all others. His self-comparison with the kings of tragedy was apt. The grand vision to which he subordinated all other considerations was no different from Oedipus' relentless quest for the murderer of Laius. Each had his moment of triumph, and each fell from eminence.

While Plato does not achieve Dion's tragic stature, he suffers no less intensely. His anguish was largely internal. First he was torn between theory and practice. Then after Dion decided to sail against Dionysius when he learned that the tyrant had disposed of his property and had given his wife in marriage to Timocrates, Plato could neither condone nor condemn his decision. Drawing on the *Seventh Epistle*, Mary Renault argues that Plato took no stand because he was still Dionysius' guest-friend; to the ancients the bond of *xenia* (guest-friendship) took precedence over personal relationships. Like a Greek chorus, Plato could only warn Dion against arrogance but was powerless to check it.

The tragedy of Plato is intimately linked with his whole system of philosophy which was never intended to leave the realm of the abstract. Of all the thinkers of antiquity, he was the most creative. In *The Mask of Apollo*, Plato is described as being more interested in the "why" of man's actions than in the "how." His pupil Aristotle will explore the "how" and consequently will never experience Plato's self-torment; catalogers rarely do because they reduce human actions to categories which are in themselves satisfying enough to prevent further questioning. One should read Plato's *Dialogues* as one reads poetry, marveling at their subtlety and language but never expecting them to yield a *modus vivendi.*

The greatest tragedy of all is that which befell Syracuse, a city that lacked a genuine aristocracy of birth and therefore should never have been selected for an experiment in constitutional monarchy with a philosopher-king. Tyrannies were common in Sicily since the sixth century B.C.; attempts at oligarchic and even democratic governments were short-lived. Even after Timoleon's reforms, Sicily no longer had the strength to use its freedom properly, and it was only a matter of time before Rome expelled the Carthaginians and absorbed the island herself.

As if by some astral determinism, the publication of *The Mask of Apollo* coincided with the escalation of the Vietnam War. Dion's folly was not unrelated to the tragic error which the United States committed in southeast Asia. Attempting to impose a so-called "superior" form of government on a country which was ideologically unequipped to accept it was little more than perverted missionary zeal, a quality Dion shared with Lyndon B. Johnson.

5

The Serpent and the Eagle: *Fire from Heaven*

" 'For I am consumed as a fire from heaven consumes a forest; how can I suffer this but from a god?' " (p. 101) Theseus exclaimed in *The Bull from the Sea* after he had seen Hippolyta. The Homeric simile perfectly objectivized Theseus' inner state. Yet after *The Bull from the Sea*, Mary Renault began to rely less on simile and more on metaphor and symbol. While Theseus compared his passion for Hippolyta to a fire from heaven, Alexander the Great, the subject of her latest novel, *is* that fire. The switch from simile to metaphor reflects a similar change in Mary Renault's development as a novelist. After the Theseus novels, she abandoned mythographic narration with its luxuriant and occasionally self-indulgent style, composite comparisons and colors that were kaleidoscopic in their range and intensity. In *The Mask of Apollo*, the Minoan sunburst palled to chiaroscuro; it had to be a style lean enough to suggest cultural emaciation. For *Fire from Heaven* (1969), she used a style that was intermediary between the lushness of *The King Must Die* and the desiccation of *The Mask of Apollo*; she could no longer return to *The Last of the Wine*'s pure Atticism, for its natural elegance would suffer *dépaysement* in fourth-century Macedonia. One has only to compare the diarist voice that opens *The Mask of Apollo* with the evocative image

that springs from the first page of *Fire from Heaven* to
see how well the author has achieved a stylistic mean:

> The child was wakened by the knotting of the snake's
> coils about his waist. For a moment he was fright-
> ened; it had squeezed his breathing, and given him a
> bad dream. But as soon as he was awake, he knew
> what it was, and pushed his two hands inside the coil.
> It shifted; the strong band under the back bunched
> tightly, then grew thin. The head slid up his shoulder
> along his neck, and he felt close to his ear the flicker-
> ing tongue.[1]

Fire from Heaven covers only the first two-thirds of
Alexander's life, from his fifth to his twentieth year. It
is the perfection of a technique that appeared inchoa-
tively in *The Middle Mist* and has been the author's
trademark since *The Charioteer*—tracing an adult's failure or success to his childhood environment. That Mary
Renault should make Alexander's boyhood the key to
his personality is not surprising, since she has been approaching characterization in this way since 1944. That
she has succeeded in spite of odds that were almost
self-defeating is another tribute to her talent for "wring-
ing lilies from the acorn."

Alexander made a brief appearance at the end of *The
Mask of Apollo*. Niko gazed at his piercing blue eyes
and knew instinctively, as only an actor could, that he
was destined for glory and suffering. Mary Renault has
isolated that suffering in a childhood where a son was
forced to choose between a bisexual father whose ambi-
tion he admired and a possessive mother whose affection
he craved. The critic who might feel the novelist is re-
peating what is now a typical Renault boyhood would be
correct; Alexander's youth could easily constitute a case
history of parental polarization, but with one essential

difference: most children facing the dilemma of divided allegiance would acquire a lasting neurosis; Alexander was a world conqueror when he died at thirty-three.

Mary Renault did not invent the facts of Alexander's scarred boyhood; history provided them, however obliquely, and the author interpreted them according to the canons of fiction. *Fire from Heaven* is her most Plutarchan novel. In the preface to his *Life of Alexander*, Plutarch admitted that his intention was not to write history, but "lives." He compared himself to the portrait painter who searches his subject's face for those subtle features and traits which can be found nowhere else. Likewise the biographer discovers that a man's exploits are often inadequate for a character sketch; "sometimes a seemingly insignificant matter, an expression or a jest are more revelatory of character than sieges or battles." Mary Renault's art is remarkably similar; she will seize upon seemingly unimportant details in her sources—a mother's obsession with the worship of Dionysus, a father's polygamous nature, a favorite horse, a beloved book like the *Iliad*—and then infer that a boy whose parents were so markedly different in temperament might gravitate to animals and literature to assuage his loneliness.

Fire from Heaven opens with Alexander asleep in his bed as a serpent knots itself around his waist. The serpent will become the symbol of the silver cord by which his mother, Olympias, has bound him to her. However, it is not an arbitrary symbol; Olympias was a princess of Epirus and proud of her heritage, although the Macedonians considered her people barbaric and uncivilized. Before her marriage to Philip, she dreamed that Zeus had impregnated her in the form of a serpent; when she was particularly enraged at her husband's infidelities, she would insinuate that Alexander was not Philip's son. Plutarch also claimed that Philip's sexual attraction for Olympias diminished because she used to bring snakes with her to bed.

Alexander's dependence on his mother prompts the same Oedipal proposal of marriage that the five-year-old Laurie made to Mrs. Odell in *The Charioteer*, but here the similarity between the two works ends. In sixteen years Mary Renault has grown as a writer; in her fiction since *The Charioteer* she has dramatized the significant events in her main character's life instead of selecting certain episodes and leaving the lacunae to the reader's imagination. In *The Charioteer*, eleven years elapsed between Laurie's declaration of marriage and the awakening of his homosexual instincts. The reader was to infer that there was a cause-effect relationship between Mrs. Odell's misdirected maternalism and her son's homosexuality; still, if one swallow does not make a summer, one marriage proposition does not make a homosexual. Although *The Charioteer* merited respect for its wisdom and compassion, one still had the disquieting feeling that the author's psychology was a trifle simplistic.

Alexander's sexual mores will always be a matter of conjecture. According to Plutarch, Alexander used to say that sex and sleep made him conscious of his mortality; but the historian then hastened to add that the statement should be interpreted to mean that both proceed from the same frail human nature. In the novel, Mary Renault leaves no doubt that there was a physical attraction between Alexander and Hephaestion. Hephaestion's furtive attempts at embracing his friend, their protestations of undying love, and their mutual joy at reading about Plato's army of lovers in the *Phaedrus* would suggest homosexuality to those unfamiliar with Greek morals. While *Fire from Heaven* is more sexually explicit than any of her previous novels, it is surprisingly discreet in the depiction of Alexander's love for

Hephaestion. In *The Last of the Wine*, one could isolate the exact moment when Alexias and Lysis consummated their love, although it was described as idyllically as the garden where it happened.

From the author's presentation, one has no other choice but to infer that Alexander and Hephaestion were far more concerned with pursuing the Greek ideal of *philia* or mutual love than sexual gratification; the latter was merely a manifestion of the former and not the end or *telos* of love between males. Alexander modeled his friendship with Hephaestion on Achilles' friendship with Patroclus. Homer, who was not beyond acknowledging the facts of life (Nestor's command that each Greek warrior lie with a Trojan wife before returning home, Hera's seduction of Zeus on Mount Ida), described the bond between Achilles and Patroclus as an emotional attachment and nothing more. Should a critic decide that they did more in the tent than sing about heroes, someone would probably endorse his theory, given the state of literary criticism today. His Achilles, however, would no longer be Homer's, but rather a synthetic creation deduced from a premise (two men alone = homosexuality) at which the Greek poet would have scoffed for its utter naïveté.

Mary Renault is equally circumspect about Alexander and Hephaestion; her refusal to give the reader The Scene suggests that the friendship played an important, but not an exclusive role in Alexander's development. In fact, their friendship is similar to the one William Maxwell described in the first half of his novel of adolescence, *The Folded Leaf* (1945), were Lymie and Spud shared their deepest thoughts, and on one occasion, a double bed but purely for warmth. No doubt someone will resurrect *The Folded Leaf* and label it the masked homosexual novel of the forties, while at the same time giving the definitive interpretation to St. John's resting his head on Christ's shoulder at the Last Supper.

What is amazing about Alexander is the speed with which his childhood scars healed. He was just short of five when he witnessed a bedroom brawl in which Olympias berated her husband for being unfaithful to her with a boy, and Philip lashed out at his wife for being a barbarian. While the incident is fictitious, it does not transcend the probable. One reason for their marital discord was Olympias' inability to accept the fact that the Macedonians expected their king to be unfaithful to his wife.

During the altercation, Alexander not only saw his father naked but in a state of erection as well. Had this happened to Laurie Odell, one could add that the sight of his father's genitals in the crucial fifth year intensified his problem. In Alexander's case, bickering left a far deeper impression than nudity. In fact, when Alexander was fifteen, he again saw his father nude, but apparently for the first time: "As far as he could remember, he had never seen him naked before" (p. 177). Alexander was spared Laurie's neurosis, although both had similar childhoods. While he sought but never really found perfect male companionship in Hephaestion and in his soldiers, the lovelessness he felt as a boy did not destroy him. Yet he never escaped the loneliness that comes when love is denied.

Equally amazing was Alexander's ability to transcend the morally ambiguous environment in which he was raised. His father was a bisexual to whom a casual affair with a boy in no way diminished his manhood. Philip did not even possess Myron's double standard in *The Last of the Wine* where homosexuality, provided it existed between lover and beloved, was morally indifferent. When he sensed the close relationship between his son and Hephaestion, he sanctioned it because he knew it was important for Alexander to have a friend's admiration. Olympias, on the other hand, loathed her husband for his pederastic amours; when she saw that

Alexander and Hephaestion were inseparable, she belittled her son in the only way she could—by challenging his virility. She cannot believe that at eighteen, Alexander has no interest in the heterosexual and criticizes him for ignoring a courtesan who entertained him one evening. When he finally sleeps with a girl whom his mother had sent to seduce him, he reminds her to inform Olympias that in the future he will choose his own lovers.

Despite his checkered sex life, Philip is anxious that his son become a "man," although Alexander spent his youth among The Companions and by the age of eight knew a few barracks terms for lovemaking. When Alexander kissed a young officer who helped him down from his horse, his uncle Lamprias promptly beat him although the boy had undoubtedly seen similar displays of affection before. Lamprias wanted a Spartan education for Alexander, a somewhat strange goal in view of the fact that Spartan discipline and homosexuality were hardly strange bedfellows. Alexander soon learned to sing to the accompaniment of the cithara; yet when he entertained the Macedonian nobles with a song, Philip became outraged at his "unmanly" behavior and forbade him to sing again. The incident which is found in Plutarch suggests that Philip was as provincial as the country he ruled. Music was an integral part of a Greek's education; Themistocles was considered a boor because he could not play the lyre. The King reminds one of the father in Robert Anderson's *Tea and Sympathy* who was ashamed to tell his friends that his son wanted to be a folk singer, which in the early fifties was not exactly the most virile of vocations.

The moral tension operating within his own family explains some of the contradictions in Alexander's personality. The King may take a boy lover for sheer lust, but his son must engage in a more aesthetic form of male devotion; Achilles sang of heroes and was no less a man for it, but Alexander must reject anything as emasculating as song. Mary Renault has answered the biographers, some of whom idealized Alexander into a dreamer who brought Greek culture wherever he went; the others drawing him as a drunken megalomaniac who treated women deferentially because he was a homosexual.

Alexander's early devotion to his mother probably led to a chivalrous attitude toward women; it is therefore understandable that he would be one of the few military leaders in history who punished the rape of female captives by death. Respect for women was not a weakness in him; it was a quality he acquired as a child and one that was obviously not shared by his father. It would be natural for Alexander to desire to surpass his father in civility and temperance.

Alexander never resolved his ambivalent feelings toward his parents. In his youth, he was always reversing his sympathies, sometimes supporting the parent he had previously defied. At five he was Olympias' son and would try to protect her from Philip's insults. Like Theseus who was something of a Lawrentian male, Alexander soon realized the dangers of female possessiveness and began to disregard his mother's suggestions. He refused to wear the jewelry she recommended and would not allow her to curl his hair. In Philip's absence, Olympias wished to receive Aristotle, but Alexander insisted it was his task to welcome the philosopher.

Although he outgrew his mother's influence, he always treated her with respect; but as usual, the waning of maternal control was accompanied by a growing identification with the father. When Philip realized Alexander's potential for kingship and Alexander understood how Philip shifted the balance of power in Greece to the side of Macedonia, a tolerable, if not ideal, union of father and son resulted. Sharing battle plans with his father was far more exciting than helping his mother select jewelry to impress some delegation. When Philip was wounded at Perinthus (Perinthos), Alexander raced after the suspected assailant and killed him. As Philip hobbled about on his disabled leg, Alexander tried to lessen his embarrassment by calling the wound a witness to his valor.

The acquisition of the horse Bucephalus (Boukephalos) is one of the best remembered stories of Alexander's youth. In Plutarch, the incident is just another tale of a *Wunderkind* who proved his elders wrong. Philip had been offered a horse that was so spirited it could not be mounted. When Alexander criticized the methods the grooms were using to break in the horse, Philip was annoyed at his son's arrogance but reluctantly let him try his hand at taming the animal. *Mirabile dictu*, the boy succeeded, for he knew that the horse's so-called viciousness was really fear of its own shadow. Turning the horse around so that it faced the sun, Alexander mounted it and rode triumphantly in full view of his father and attendants.

In the novel, the episode is important not so much as a manifestation of Alexander's practical sense which was evident when he entertained the Persian ambassadors at the age of seven, but rather as the first occasion when Philip and Alexander behaved as father and son. Mary Renault saw in the Plutarchan anecdote the generational conflict between an obdurate father and a clever son, each of whom firmly believed in his own position. The dialogue catches the resentment, tension and humor of a son's coaxing his father to make a wager which he knows full well will turn out in his favor. The boy also changes the horse's name from Thunder to Oxhead, the literal translation of Bucephalus. Alexander was always concerned about names. Because kings could rarely recall the names of their soldiers, he resolved to know each of his men personally. As an adolescent, Alexander realized that animals, like humans, have no other choice but to live up to the titles they have been given. One only calls a horse Thunder if one expects it to be recalcitrant.

When Philip decided to take another wife, Alexander was sympathetic; he had come to realize something about the middle-aged male's need for reassurance from a younger woman. At the wedding feast, the bride's father proposed a toast that a legitimate heir might come from the marriage. Alexander, who was always dubious about his origins, left in a rage and took his mother back to Epirus.

The episode is historically accurate. Philip did marry the niece of his general, Attalus (Attalos); her name was Cleopatra, but in the novel she is called by her honorific Eurydice (Eurydike) so that she would not be confused with Alexander's sister of the same name. While the banquet scene has an almost operatic flamboyance (particularly Alexander's flinging a wine cup at Attalus), it brings back all the ambivalence and doubts of his childhood. Naturally Alexander would react violently to an insinuation of illegitimacy; since he was twelve, he considered himself his father's son. Attalus' drunken toast drove him back to Olympias; although he will return to Pella, Philip and Alexander will never share another moment of genuine affection as they did when they embraced after the taming of Bucephalus.

Although one may be tempted to regard Alexander's youth as tragic, Mary Renault does not depict it from that point of view. *Fire from Heaven* does not approach the cosmic level of *The Mask of Apollo* where political reform brought only bloodshed and disenchantment. To the Stoics and Peripatetics, Alexander was an example of fortune's fickleness; his death from a fever when he was on the threshold of world dominion may strike one as lamentable in the sense that there was no eleventh-hour reprieve. Alexander's youth would have been tragic had he succumbed to self-pity and allowed the polarized household to destroy him.

At the end of the novel, Alexander sees a golden eagle clutching a snake in its talons. The powerful image is Homeric, but in the *Iliad* (12. 200 ff.), the snake strikes the eagle in the breast; the eagle, writhing in pain, drops the snake and flies off. In *Fire from Heaven*, the snake struggles to free itself, but the eagle spirals into the heavens until he and his prey are lost from sight. The novel which began with Olympias' snake entwined around the sleeping Alexander ends with a serpent trapped in an eagle's talons. The eagle, the sacred bird of Zeus, was a symbol of masculinity. With his father's murder and his mother's loss of authority, Alexander has finally sloughed off the influence of his parents. The serpent and the eagle have vanished above the mountain peaks.

Fire from Heaven was clearly designed to be the companion novel to *The Mask of Apollo*. Thettalos reappears as a secret agent, a function actors often performed in the fourth century; and Niko comforts him after a near escape from death. Should anyone wish to know whatever became of Dionysius II, the intended philosopher-king, he had to support himself by taking in students at Corinth. Also common to both novels is Euripides' *Bacchae*, a play which interested Mary Renault since *Return to Night* where it was one of Julian Fleming's favorites. It was not until *The King Must Die* that she could incorporate the cult of Dionysus into a novel.

In *The Mask of Apollo*, the *Bacchae* symbolized the divided city of Syracuse. That Pentheus' mask should resemble Dion was poetic justice; like Pentheus, Dion also advocated a policy which found favor with no one else. In *Fire from Heaven*, the *Bacchae* is linked with the character of Olympias and the impression she left on the young Alexander. Mary Renault has accepted Plutarch's thesis that Olympias brought the Dionysian worship with her from Epirus. During the ritual, she would dance with tame serpents wrapped around her. The culminating act of worship was the dismemberment of an animal. However, there are records of human sacrifice, and it is interesting to note that on one occasion Olympias used the ritual as a means of ridding herself of a rival for Philip's affections.

When he was five, Alexander saw his mother lead the rites. Three years later, he attended a performance of the *Bacchae* in which his mother appeared much to the astonishment of the audience. Traditionally, the same actor who played Pentheus also impersonated Agave, but on this occasion Olympias herself stepped into the part of the mother maddened by religious frenzy. Apart from the unprecedented appearance of a woman on stage, her performance is a votive offering to the god she worshipped, the culmination of a series of ritual actions that included black magic and imprecations by which she hoped to punish Philip for his infidelities. The *Bacchae*, as Niko observed, is a play about mystery— the mystery of man who is part spirit and part matter, the mystery of society which is the divided self in enlarged form. In *Fire from Heaven*, the drama is a metaphor for Alexander's childhood which was also a tug-of-war between emotion (Olympias) and reason (Philip).

In the past, Mary Renault's approach to historical fiction consisted of inventing one or two main characters and drawing the rest of her cast from actual figures of antiquity. *Fire from Heaven* is her first historical novel in which the main character is not fictitious. Yet it has always been the author's purpose to introduce men of letters into the plot, partly in an effort to rescue them from bibliographical oblivion and provide them with the third dimension which the textbooks never supplied. In *Fire from Heaven*, Mary Renault has dusted off Aristotle and Demosthenes and revealed them in all their fallible splendor.

From a historical viewpoint, the philosopher and the orator were logical choices. Aristotle was Alexander's most successful tutor, and Demosthenes' antagonism to Philip was well known. In his *Philippics*, Demosthenes kept trying to convince the Athenians that the rise of Macedonia would diminish their own power. Depicting Philip as a barbarian who threatened Greece and her gods, Demosthenes turned the prospect of a united Macedonia into the specter of Athenian enslavement.

In researching *Fire from Heaven*, Mary Renault examined the speeches of Demosthenes and cut through the jungle of scholarship that had grown up around them. She has concluded that by our standards they are little more than brilliantly worded agitprop. She also examined Plutarch's *Life of Demosthenes* where she read that in his youth the great orator was nicknamed "Batalus." However, Plutarch is uncertain about the etymology of the nickname. As is his custom, he suggests a few (the name of an effeminate flute player, a writer of lascivious poems and drinking songs) and then remarks that "Athenians called a certain part of the body which one should not mention by name *batalos*."

Actually, we have no idea what *batalos* means; the etymologies have ranged from "mama's boy" to "stammerer." However, in the fourth century the word must have had a homosexual connotation. In his oration *Against Timarchus*, Aeschines claims that Demosthenes, whom he sneeringly calls "the graduate of the wrestling school," was called *batalos* because of his effeminate behavior and homosexual propensities. Using the little linguistic evidence that is available plus Aeschines' allegations, Mary Renault has inferred that the nickname meant one who was easily aroused by the presence of his own sex: "He had been a puny lad, exciting no one's desire but readily excited; in the boys' gymnasium this had been starkly exposed, and the dirty nickname had stuck to him for years" (p. 88).

In *Fire from Heaven*, Demosthenes first appears as one of the ten Athenian envoys sent to negotiate a peace with Philip. The episode is partly factual, for such an embassy did visit Pella toward the end of 347 B.C.; Demosthenes and his archenemy, Aeschines, were among the ambassadors. Aeschines, an actor turned orator, states with some degree of veracity in *On the Embassy* that Demosthenes was to speak last; but when his turn arrived, he became so nervous and inarticulate that he could not remember his speech.

Mary Renault has worked fact and anecdote into the episode. In the novel, both orators are forced to share a room in Philip's palace. Demosthenes, who was always in poor health, complains of the accommodations, the cold, his sore throat, and even the inaccessibility of the chamber pot. When he recalls how Aeschines made sly remarks about his grandfather's marriage to a Scythian, he mutters: " 'You were an usher, I was a student; you were an acolyte, I was an initiate; you copied the minutes, I moved the motion; you were third actor, I sat in front' " (p. 87).

Readers of Demosthenes' famous speech, *On the Crown*, will remember a similar passage where the orator contrasted his public life with Aeschines':

You taught reading; I attended school. You conducted initiations into the mysteries; I was actually initiated. You were a clerk, I a member of the assembly. You were third actor, I a spectator. You used to be booed; I hissed. Your public life was spent for the good of our enemies, mine for the good of our country.

Although *On the Crown* was not delivered until seventeen years after the embassy to Pella, it is not inconceivable that Demosthenes wrote down that brilliant piece of isocolon he muttered in the novel and waited for an opportunity to insert it in a speech. According to Plutarch, "Demosthenes was always correcting, transforming and rephrasing whatever others said to him, or he to them." What is amusing is the fact that Demosthenes thought in the same paratactical style in which he wrote.

Niko's final thought in *The Mask of Apollo* was about the tragedy that results when two great men never meet because they miss each other by a few decades: "No one will ever make a tragedy—and that is as well, for one could not bear it—whose grief is that the principals never met" (p. 321). The principals were, of course, Plato and Alexander. Perhaps with Alexander, Plato could have realized his ideal of a philosopher-king. His student, Aristotle, did not have such lofty aspirations. While he admired his teacher, Aristotle never accepted the Doctrine of Forms and wrote his *Poetics* partly in answer to Plato's theory of art. As a married man, Aristotle felt somewhat superior to the bachelor Plato. Aristotle's views on education would differ greatly from Plato's: "Nature had no mysteries, only facts not yet correctly observed and analyzed" (p. 163). One can only speculate how Alexander would have fared under Plato's tutelage (he would still have conquered the world but would have been more introspective about it); but the training Aristotle brought with him, the scientific combined with the humanistic, was more in keeping with Alexander's character.

Aristotle did not begin Alexander's education with geometry as Plato would have done; rather he exposed his pupil to a broad spectrum of knowledge including natural science, optics, logic, law, ethics, and the explication of literature. Soon his appetite for learning knew no limits. Alexander became an admirer of Xenophon, particularly his *Cyropaedia* (called *The Upbringing of Cyrus* in the novel), a work which Mary Renault believes had a profound effect on him. In fact, she is surprised that scholars never detected its influence. Certainly when Alexander reflected on Xenophon's thesis that a ruler must be able to cast a spell over his subjects, he must have realized that a spell would only be effective if the ruler were regarded as divine.

All of Alexander's qualities—his desire to play Achilles to Hephaestion's Patroclus, his devotion to Hercules, his interest in literature that expressed the ideals of archaic Greece, and his nascent Aristotelianism that caused him to exclaim " 'The soul must live to *do*' " (p. 212)—would seem to suggest an ascetic. There was a mystical side to his nature which perhaps the sequel to *Fire from Heaven* will disclose. If the Theseus novels are any guide, the author should continue the story of Alexander from his accession to his death. In *Fire from Heaven,* she is presenting Alexander as a Hercules-Cyrus-Achilles composite; she is also implying that his extension of Hellenic culture to Asia was the result of his ability to blend the lessons of the past with the needs of the present. For Alexander, the past was not food on which one fed vicariously; it was a living entity whose ideals are always realizable.

Although *Fire from Heaven* is biographically incomplete, it heralds a new approach to historical fiction on the author's part. Her first four explorations of Greek civilization were formation novels in the tradition of *The Charioteer*. While her main concern was the effect of environment on character, her method admitted of several variations. Not every boy who grew up without the stabilizing influence of a father sought to recover his loss in a homosexual friendship. Laurie and Alexias did, but in different ways—Laurie by accepting the inevitable liaison with Ralph, Alexias by embracing a Platonism that gave dignity to male love. Theseus was also a fatherless child, but he found a surrogate in a deity. To a modern, Theseus' masculine bravado might suggest fear of homosexuality; yet if he ever had any such fears, they could easily be allayed by the limitless range of exploits the Heroic Age had to offer. A fatherless male may need a woman to banish self-doubt (Mic in *Promise of Love*, Julian in *Return to Night*); or he may live in a society where a woman's love is unnecessary for the achievement of excellence (Niko in *The Mask of Apollo*).

Alexander provides a solution to the question of masculinity that haunts Mary Renault's fiction. While Theseus divinized his virility, Alexander divinized himself. Theseus' Poseidon was a god limited in both jurisdiction (the sea) and appetite (sex). Alexander chose as his models Hercules, who underwent twelve labors to achieve the status of demigod; Achilles, whose preference for short-lived glory instead of undistinguished longevity became the basis of his own life; and Cyrus the Great, whose idealized education in Xenophon's *Cyropaedia* may very well have given Alexander the idea of a divine monarch.

Fire from Heaven is Mary Renault's first Hellenic novel not written in the first person. The memoir form has gone, and with it the artistic problems that result when omniscience vacillates between neutral and editorial. The author was wise in abandoning "I narration" for a book about Alexander; the reminiscence technique worked satisfactorily in the other Greek novels, since Alexias and Niko were fictitious characters and Theseus was mythological. It would not work in a novel about one of the greatest military geniuses in history; one would expect him to explain his own greatness and answer the questions that scholars have posed since Plutarch's time. Furthermore, it is Mary Renault's contention that Alexander really never knew himself; he knew only the dream which he imbibed from Homer and which he pushed to its geographical limits.

Fire from Heaven is a new novel for Mary Renault in other respects. It contains far less of the supernatural than anything she has written thus far; there are no bargains struck with deities, no dialogues with masks. While the Dionysian ritual occurs twice, its purpose is to deepen the character of Olympias, who was not beyond resorting to magic and murder to gain her ends, rather than to provide an otherworldly atmosphere which a novel about Alexander the Great certainly does not need. The author also makes no attempt to idealize the battle scenes; they are presented in all of their Homeric detachment. When Alexander kills his first man at the age of twelve, the nausea he feels is intensified when someone suggests he may have slain another as well. During a campaign, a nursing mother rushes up to him after her baby was killed. After Chaeronia (Chaironia), he surveys the dead; he recognizes one of the men he had killed but is uncertain about another. Alexander has become inured to war and death.

Mary Renault has written a novel where spears pierce windpipes, wounds gape and hiss, horses fall to the ground with their riders, and heads are dispassionately severed from corpses. Despite the emphasis on violence, the writing never loses its epic objectivity. Because it reflects Alexander's point of view, *Fire from Heaven* cannot be considered antiwar. In an effort to make ancient literature relevant, some professors have turned the *Iliad* into a pacifist poem which it clearly is not; it was only through war that the Homeric hero could win *kudos*. In the case of *Fire from Heaven*, such an approach would also be historically invalid. Whether or not it offends one's sensibilities, Alexander was a man who could only achieve his destiny through war and conquest. To see him in any other light would vitiate the facts of history for which Mary Renault has great respect.

That the novel remained so long on the best-seller list is perhaps the greatest tribute to the author's achievement. *Fire from Heaven* is a difficult book to read, for Mary Renault has written it on her own terms, as the Author's Note indicates. There are more proper names than usual and, of course, they are not latinized. Even a student versed in ancient literature might blink his eyes at a reference to Euripides' *Bakchai*, a spelling that admittedly slows down one's speed. However, those who read *War and Peace* or *Crime and Punishment* in the days when there were no review books to give a pronunciation guide should not have a major problem. "Make haste slowly," as Augustus used to say.

Peter Wolfe closed his study of Mary Renault with an attempt to explain the reluctance of critics to give her the same serious consideration accorded some of her contemporaries. Like Mary McCarthy, Truman Capote, and Gore Vidal, Mary Renault has attracted journalists rather than critics; like them she is also "commercially successful," a phrase that conjures up the names of Kathleen Winsor, Taylor Caldwell, and Grace Metalious. Wolfe also argued that "the prevailing critical animus against homosexual fiction and historical fiction has already delayed the recognition she deserves," [2] a statement that does not speak well for the so-called impartiality of our men of letters.

"Homosexual fiction" is a rather general term. When a novel is labeled homosexual, one presumes it is about homosexuals and written from their point of view (John Rechy's *City of Night* and *Numbers*, Hubert Selby, Jr.'s *Last Exit to Brooklyn*). There are also novels in which a character's homosexuality is underplayed for social or artistic reasons (Gide's *The Immoralist*, Proust's *Remembrance of Things Past*, Colette's *Claudine Married*); as a result, the work attracts a heterogeneous audience that finds its literary merits more important than its sexual philosophy. Lastly, there is homosexual fiction, overt or disguised, written by homosexuals—a category which the 1960s with its penchant for classifying authors like butterflies "pinned and wriggling on the wall" has devised for the voyeurs the decade has spawned.

There is no critical law, nor should there be, about the use of homosexuality in literature, but there is one caveat for the writer who chooses this theme; novels like John Rechy's which minutely examine the homosexual demimonde invite criticism that is more sociological than literary. Such books, in their attempt to be honest, often become maudlin, especially if the main character is a quixotic soul in quest of the ideal relationship. Yet Wolfe is correct in questioning a critical approach that sees no distinction between homosexual novelists, novels about homosexuality, and novels that use homosexuality as a plot device. Jean Genet's *Our Lady of the Flowers*, Gore Vidal's *The City and the Pillar*, and James Baldwin's *Another Country* are thematically light years removed from *The Last of the Wine* and should be evaluated according to the genres they represent. Mary Renault writes historical fiction and should be judged according to its canons.

It is impossible to imagine a novel about ancient Greece which does not consider its sexual ethic; had Mary Renault discreetly skirted the issue, one of her astute reviewers like Rex Warner or Orville Prescott would have blamed the omission on Victorian prudery which the author certainly does not possess. As it is, her use of homosexuality is a perfect illustration of the Thomistic principle of integrity, or rendered in less aesthetic terms, "the whole is equal to the sum of its consecutive parts." A novel about Greek males in the fourth century B.C. would have to take into account the bisexual culture; otherwise it would be historically incomplete.

In the long run, it is the academicians who apotheosize an author. Their preferences have rarely coincided with the *New York Review of Books* or the *New York Times Book Review*, but their tastes are reflected in the literary journals and in reading lists for contemporary literature courses. In one sense, their power is more awesome than a reviewer's; a journalist can give a novel a transient renown, but a professor can insure its immortality by his lectures and books.

In the case of Mary Renault, Academe has discovered an anomaly. Theoretically, it should be up to the classicists to promote her work; but literary criticism is still unknown to many teachers of Latin and Greek who spend so much time mastering the languages that they have little patience with anything that is not philological. Unfortunately, many share A. E. Housman's sentiments which he expressed in his 1911 Cambridge Inaugural: "That a scholar should appreciate literature is good for his own pleasure and profit; but it is none of his business to communicate that appreciation to his audience." It is only recently that American classicists have begun to apply the critical theories of Blackmur, Richards, Wellek and Warren, Frye, et al. to ancient literature to the extent that a critical vocabulary is discernible in some of their studies. Yet except for an occasional course in Greek Civilization or Mythology, the classicist who believes that Mary Renault's value goes beyond background reading would be hard pressed to find another way to acquaint his students with her work.

On the other hand, English professors, who feel sufficiently qualified to teach World Literature or Greek Tragedy in Translation, would probably want a "specialist" to evaluate a Mary Renault novel; yet the specialist would be more concerned about the technical aspects of Greek culture than he would be about the accuracy of a historical novel. However, few professors of literature would feel ill-prepared to discuss works like O'Neill's *Mourning Becomes Electra*, Anouilh's *Eurydice*, Giraudoux's *Tiger at the Gates*, and Butor's *Passing Time*, all of which require only a nodding acquaintance with mythology; as mythic literature, they demand the analysis of a littérateur, not the commentary of a scholiast. Because Mary Renault is the only novelist of quality writing about antiquity, she is doomed to share the plight of the Classics in the university—admired but unencouraged.

Critical indifference to Mary Renault is partly the result of a compartmentalized university system where only specialists are expected to review and discuss authoritatively works in their field; in the author's case this meant reviews by Gilbert Highet, Rex Warner, and the late Moses Hadas, all eminently qualified critics. Yet it should be noted that the very first article on Mary Renault was written not by a classicist, but by a "specialist" in modern fiction, Landon C. Burns, who was equally at home with Stephen Crane and Henry James. His essay was not only the first attempt to consider Mary Renault as a serious writer; it was also a distinguished piece of literary criticism in its own right. Anyone who read some of the ancient historians in English, especially Herodotus and Plutarch, would be able to appreciate her concept of fiction and write intelligently about it. Even Miss Renault does her research primarily from translations.

Wolfe is also correct in blaming the neglect of Mary Renault on the condescending attitude of modern criticism to historical fiction. The mythic novel has achieved literary status because it is receptive to the theories of Freud, Frazer, Jung, Bodkin, and Eliade. The mythological novel is still treated like a stepchild because critics do not expect a novel set in antiquity to have any art. The mythic novel is Jungian; the mythological is *Märchen*.

The modern critics, however, are only partly at fault. The distinction between the mimetic (fiction in the broadest sense of the word) and the nonmimetic (history) dates back to Aristotle. In the *Poetics*, Aristotle made his famous distinction between history and tragedy; for the sake of the argument one can consider tragedy as serious literature in general. Art that imitates (poetry, drama, the novel) is superior to art that relates (history, chronicle). History relates what has happened, literature what may or will happen. Literature expresses the universal, not the particulars; it discloses what is unchangeable in human nature, not merely the variables in an individual's life. History is concerned with facts; literature transforms facts into truth. In fiction, events are linked causally and sequentially; in history, events are strung together without any clearly defined connection.

Like most distinctions, Aristotle's is an oversimplification; for one thing, Aeschylus' *Persians*, the only extant historical Greek tragedy, is never mentioned in the *Poetics*. Obviously Aristotle would never illustrate his rules with exceptions. As a result of the emphasis he put on the structural perfection of *Oedipus the King*, students for centuries looked upon the Sophoclean drama as the most representative of the Greek tragedies, which it is not. Euripides' *Bacchae*, which is much better known today because it provided Golding with a point of departure for *Lord of the Flies*, comes much closer to explaining what the handbooks call "The Greek Genius" and its tragic sense of man's bipolar nature. It is very possible that the critical apathy to historical fiction derives from Aristotle's inability to envision a genre that would cut across the mimetic and the nonmimetic.

Prophesying the fate of any living writer requires a Delphic ambiguity. Anyone who witnessed T. S. Eliot's demotion from dean of modern poetry to assistant registrar soon learned to curb his Pythian tongue. Literary predictions are particularly hazardous today when social pressures make the arts more of a luxury than a necessity. How well novelists who re-create an era as removed in time as ancient Greece will fare in the next decades is difficult to say. It does seem certain that Mary Renault will maintain her literate following, for despite the prophecies of McLuhan and Vidal, the bliss of total illiteracy is too simple an answer to the problems of our civilization.

Yet any history of the contemporary novel that does not acknowledge the contribution of Mary Renault is incomplete. She has shown that historical fiction can be artistically successful when the novelist combines interpretation and invention in the right proportions. By immersing herself in a world which most readers regard with a cinematic awe, she has so thoroughly assimilated the classical vision of life, love, war, and death that her fiction is like collateral reading to Greek literature. She is also a scholar who makes important contributions to our knowledge of antiquity with every novel she writes. However critics will choose to regard her work, it is unassailably clear that Mary Renault is one of the most creative historical novelists of our era and the only bona fide Hellenist in twentieth-century fiction.

1 — The Hospital World

1. "Books," *Notes on Life and Letters* (New York: Doubleday, 1921), p. 6.

2. *Promise of Love* (New York: Popular Library, n.d.), p. 92. All subsequent references are to this edition.

3. The English title was more accurate, for it was derived from the hospital prayer which the nurses said daily. Like most ritual formulae, the noble intentions of the prayer were lost somewhere in the mindless recitation.

4. On this and related meanings of *arete*, see G. M. A. Grube, *Plato's Thought* (Boston: Beacon Paperbacks, 1958), pp. 217, 231.

5. The last two chapters are the most important in the novel, yet the anonymous *TLS* reviewer (25 February 1939, p. 119) felt it would have been a better book "if the last chapter were eliminated." The same reviewer was also a bit shocked by the "sordid" details of the love affair.

6. *Kind Are Her Answers* (New York: William Morrow, 1940), p. 32. All subsequent references are to this edition.

7. *Spectator*, 31 May 1940, p. 758.

8. *New Yorker*, 24 February 1945, p. 73.

9. *The Middle Mist* (New York: William Morrow, 1945), p. 4. All subsequent references are to this edition.

10. *New Statesman and Nation*, 14 October 1944, p. 256.

11. *Spectator*, 1 September 1944, p. 206.

12. René Wellek and Austin Warren, *Theory of Literature*, 3d ed. (New York: Harcourt, Brace & World, 1962), p. 92.

13. Henry Reed summed up the author's problem quite succinctly: "Miss Renault is at the difficult stage of being able to express subtle thoughts and truths about personalities without being able always to attach them to personalities whom they fit."

14. Grube, *Plato's Thought*, p. 90, n. 2.

15. *Return to Night* (New York: William Morrow, 1947), p. 71. All subsequent references are to this edition.

16. The film version was never made. In 1947 a combination of adultery, pseudohomosexuality, bigamy, and literate dialogue would have overwhelmed even Metro-Goldwyn-Mayer.

17. Charles Lee in the *New York Times*, 20 April 1947, p. 4.

18. *North Face* (New York: William Morrow, 1948), p. 2. All subsequent references are to this edition.

19. *Saturday Review of Literature*, 25 September 1948, p. 11.

2—*Eros and Clio*: The Charioteer *and* The Last of the Wine

1. *The Charioteer* (New York: Pocket Books, 1967), p. 12. All subsequent references are to this edition.

2. *The Last of the Wine* (New York: Pocket Books, 1964), p. 3. All subsequent references are to this edition.

3. For the critical term "narrator-agent," see Wayne C. Booth, *The Rhetoric of Fiction* (Chicago: University of Chicago, 1961), pp. 153–54.

4. Hans Licht, *Sexual Life in Ancient Greece*, trans. Freese and Dawson (New York: Barnes & Noble, 1953), p. 439.

5. Xenophon, *Memorabilia* I. 2. 30.

6. From an unpublished letter addressed from Cape, South Africa and dated August 3, 1969.

7. *Oeconomicus* 7. 23.

8. *Memorabilia* I. 6. 13.

9. Ibid., I. 3. 13.

10. On the title's change-death-loss symbolism, see Landon C. Burns, Jr., "Men Are Only Men: The Novels of Mary Renault," *Critique*, 6 (1963–64), 108.

3—To Be a King: The Theseus Novels

1. Jane Ellen Harrison, *Themis: A Study of the Social Origins of Greek Religion* (New York: Meridian Books, 1962), pp. 150–57.

2. *The King Must Die* (New York: Pocket Books, 1959), p. 6. All subsequent references are to this edition.

3. Cedric H. Whitman, *Homer and the Heroic Tradition* (Cambridge, Mass.: Harvard University Press, 1958), p. 223.

4. The best study on the subject is that of George E. Mylonas, *Eleusis and the Eleusinian Mysteries* (Princeton: Princeton University Press, 1961).

5. Robert Graves, *The Greek Myths* (Baltimore: Penguin Books, 1955), 1:332.

6. *The Bull of Minos* (New York: Universal Library, 1962), p. 117.

7. Peter Wolfe, *Mary Renault* (New York: Twayne, 1969), p. 163.

8. *The Bull from the Sea* (New York: Pocket Books, 1963), p. 10. All subsequent references are to this edition.

9. Graves, *The Greek Myths*, 1:355. Mary Renault also argues for this etymology in "Amazons," *Greek Heritage*, 1 (Spring 1964), 21.

4—The Gathering Dusk: The Mask of Apollo

1. *The Mask of Apollo* (New York: Pocket Books, 1967), p. 9. All subsequent references are to this edition.

2. In *An Apology for Poetry*, Sidney claimed that Plato was criticizing the abuse of poetry, not poetry itself. Most scholars today follow E. A. Havelock (*Preface to Plato*), who argued that the philosopher was opposed only to an oral tradition, not to poetry per se.

5—*The Serpent and the Eagle:* Fire from Heaven

1. *Fire from Heaven* (New York: Popular Library, 1969), p. 7. All subsequent references are to this edition.
2. Peter Wolfe, *Mary Renault* (New York: Twayne, 1969), p. 163.

Selected Bibliography

The Works of Mary Renault

NOVELS

Promise of Love. New York: William Morrow, 1939.
Kind Are Her Answers. New York: William Morrow, 1940.
The Middle Mist. New York: William Morrow, 1945.
Return to Night. New York: William Morrow, 1947.
North Face. New York: William Morrow, 1948.
The Last of the Wine. New York: Pantheon Books, 1956.
The King Must Die. New York: Pantheon Books, 1958.
The Charioteer. New York: Pantheon Books, 1959.
The Bull from the Sea. New York: Pantheon Books, 1962.
The Mask of Apollo. New York: Pantheon Books, 1966.
Fire from Heaven. New York: Pantheon Books, 1969.

CHILDREN'S BOOK

*The Lion in the Gateway: The Heroic Battles of the Greeks
    and Persians at Marathon, Salamis and Thermopylae.*
    Ed. by Walter Lord. New York: Harper & Row, 1964.

ESSAYS

"Amazons," *Greek Heritage,* 1 (Spring 1964), 18–23.
"Notes on *The King Must Die,*" *Afterwords: Novelists on*

Their Novels. Ed. by Thomas McCormack. New York: Harper & Row, 1969, pp. 81–87.

SECONDARY SOURCES

Burns, Landon C., Jr., "Men Are Only Men: The Novels of Mary Renault," *Critique*, 6 (1963–64), 102–21.
Wolfe, Peter. *Mary Renault*. New York: Twayne, 1969.

Index

Achilles: as model for Theseus, 58–60
Aegeus: myth of, 62–63
Aeneid: Renault's use of, 27–28
Aeschines: as historical figure, 112–13; as character in *Fire from Heaven*, 113
Aeschylus, 89, 123
Against Timarchus, 112
Ainsworth, William, xiii
Alcibiades, 45, 51
Alexander the Great: in *The Mask of Apollo*, 97; in *Fire from Heaven*, 101–10; relationship with Hephaestion, 104; as Stoic *exemplum*, 109–10; as Aristotle's pupil, 115
Amazons: in myth, 79
Anabasis, 45
Anytus (Anytos): as character in *The Last of the Wine*, 53
Apollo, 81, 89
Arete: Greek concept of, 8–9
Ariadne: as character in *The King Must Die*, 67–69
Ariadne auf Naxos, 68
Aristophanes, 88
Aristotle: as character in *Fire from Heaven*, 114–15; on history and tragedy, 122–23
Artemis, 72, 81

Atalanta in Calydon, 73
Auden, W. H.: quoted, 79

Bacchae: in *Return to Night*, 24; in *The King Must Die*, 68–69; in *The Mask of Apollo*, 92; in *Fire from Heaven*, 110–11; as source of *Lord of the Flies*, 123
Bacchus and Ariadne, 69
Balade de Bon Conseil, 27
Baldwin, James, 119
Ben Hur, 57
Binyon, Laurence, 72
Boys in the Band, The, 34
Brooke, Rupert, 13
Bucephalus (Boukephalos): taming of, 108–9
Bull from the Sea, The: discussed, 70–85; as sequel to *The King Must Die*, 70; theory of kingship in, 75, 83; compared with *Hippolytus*, 81–82, 84–85; mentioned, 31, 38, 60, 64, 69, 86, 97
Burgess, Anthony, xi
Burns, Landon C., 121

Caldwell, Taylor, xii, 118
Centaur, The, 73
Centaurs: in myth and art, 73–74
Cercyon. *See* Kerkyon